Paul Atterbury's Railway Collection

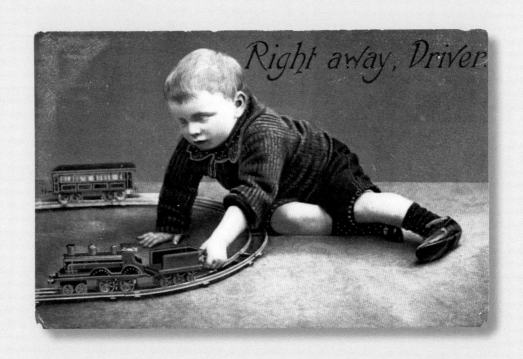

A DAVID & CHARLES BOOK
F&W Media International, Ltd 2012

David & Charles is an imprint of
F&W Media International, Ltd
Brunel House, Forde Close, Newton Abbot, TQ12 4PU, UK

F&W Media International, Ltd is a subsidiary of
F+W Media Inc.
10151 Carver Road, Cincinnati OH45242, USA

First published in the UK in 2012
Digital edition published in 2012

ISBN-13: 978-1-4463-0202-6
ISBN-10: 1-4463-0202-4

Hardback edition printed in China by RR Donnelley for:
F&W Media International, Ltd
Brunel House, Forde Close, Newton Abbot, TQ12 4PU, UK

10 9 8 7 6 5 4 3 2 1

Produced for F&W Media International, Ltd by:
OutHouse Publishing
Shalbourne, Marlborough, Wiltshire SN8 3QJ

For OutHouse Publishing:
Project editor: Sue Gordon
Art editor: Dawn Terrey
Image scanning and presentation: Chrissie Atterbury

For David & Charles:
Senior editor: Verity Muir
Art editor: Sarah Underhill
Production manager: Beverley Richardson

F+W Media publishes high-quality books on a wide
range of subjects. For more great book ideas visit:
www.rubooks.co.uk

▶ A night scene at
London's Paddington
station in March 1939 as
the 10.15pm to Weymouth
is ready to depart from
Platform 2, headed
by a GWR Star Class
locomotive, No. 4022,
'Belgian Monarch'.

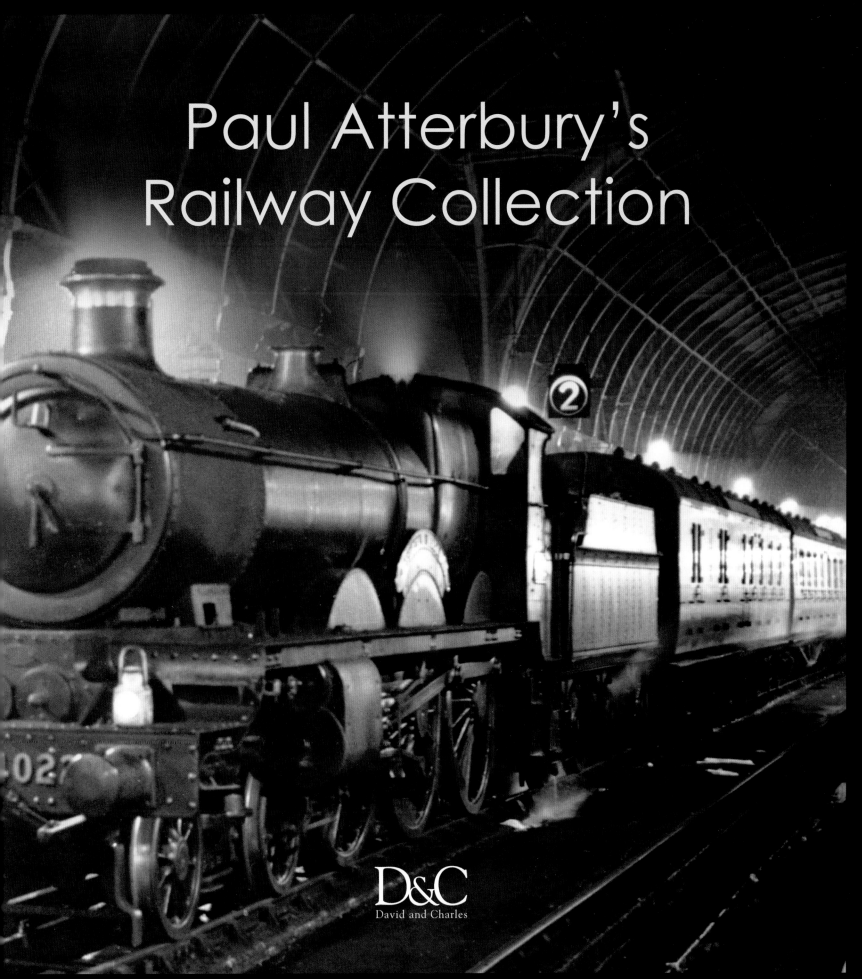

Paul Atterbury's Railway Collection

D&C
David and Charles

CONTENTS

THE BRIGHTON BELLE / THE BOURNEMO

TH BELLE

PULLMAN luxury – all the year round

INTRODUCTION

THIS BOOK is a personal collection of photographs, postcards and printed ephemera – documents that are the living records of Britain's railway history. The contents, arranged by region and interspersed with feature sections, cover the country and highlight themes and subjects that particularly interest or excite me. I know that many share my fascination with railways, and I hope that this book gives pleasure as it celebrates the wonderful visual legacy of Britain's railway past.

◀ The publicity brochures issued by British Railways are endlessly varied, and the graphics often amuse me. In 1974 someone came up with the idea of educational outings for schools. The fierce schoolmistress was perhaps a bit too persuasive!

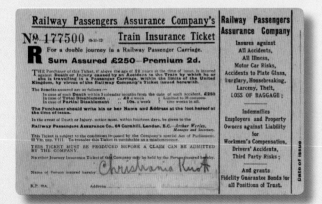

▲ Postcards with comic or romantic railway themes are common, and I always find them entertaining. I fear the answer to the sad-looking lady's question on this one, posted in 1908, is likely to be 'never'.

▲ Railway-related paperwork is intriguing in both its abundance and its content. In 1912 Christiania Knott signed up for this passenger's insurance policy paying £250 in the event of her death.

▲ In 1963 the LB&SCR Class A1 Terrier tank locomotive 'Waddon' was given by British Railways to the Canadian Railway Museum, now Exporail. This official BR photograph shows the immaculate locomotive being loaded for shipment.

▲ A classic railway scene: this postcard shows two fine Gresley LNER locomotives, an A4 and an A1, leaving King's Cross side by side.

▲ The Atlantic Coast Express, which at its peak included coaches for nine destinations, was the Southern Region's most exciting train, and one of my favourites. This shows it at speed near Plymouth, shortly before it was withdrawn in 1964.

▲ I find studio portraits of Victorian railwaymen particularly appealing, as they often reveal the sitter's pride in the job and the uniform. This example, probably from the 1880s, shows a smartly dressed GNR employee from the Melton Mowbray area.

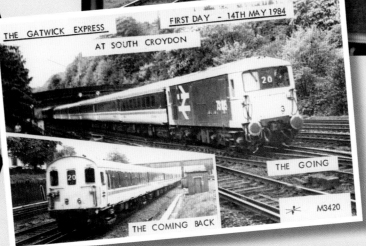

▲ This photograph, showing a signalman's view of an approaching GWR express, is anonymous and undated, but it has a place in my collection simply because it is so evocative.

▲ Railway companies have always been keen on commemorating special events and dates. I like this postcard because the first day of the Gatwick Express in 1984 must, even then, have been of relatively minor interest. It shows an original Class 73 push-pull unit and the InterCity livery used for the first few years.

GWR
Great Malvern to
Leeds

Paul's scrapbook

Tracks of my life

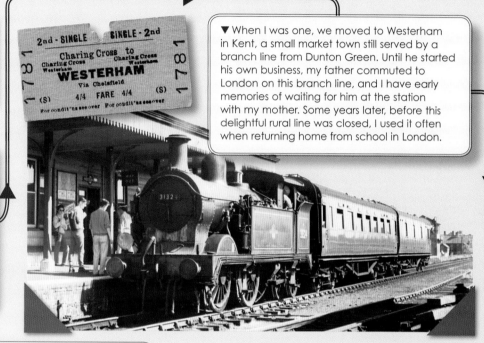

▼ When I was one, we moved to Westerham in Kent, a small market town still served by a branch line from Dunton Green. Until he started his own business, my father commuted to London on this branch line, and I have early memories of waiting for him at the station with my mother. Some years later, before this delightful rural line was closed, I used it often when returning home from school in London.

▲ My personal journey starts at the very end of World War II in Hampstead, where my mother and I lived in a flat while my father was still in the RAF. Naturally, I have no memory of this but, having no car, we were certainly regular users of Hampstead Underground station, on the Edgware branch of the Northern Line. Some years later, after my parents separated, my mother moved back to this part of north London, and once again Hampstead and Highgate Underground stations were to play an important role in my life.

▼ This is Trefeddian Terrace, Aberdovey, where I was sent with some family friends while my parents went to France. It was a pretty lonely experience for a five-year-old, but made bearable by regular train postcards, like the one on the left. The house faced the beach, across the Cambrian Coast main line. Trains passed day and night and, with little to do, I watched them all the time. I remember long goods trains, double-headed passenger expresses, and the sounds they made. This was the start of my lifelong enthusiasm for railways.

ELMSTEAD WOODS

▲ As a fairly typical small boy, I became a keen trainspotter and hours were spent standing on platforms with notebook and Ian Allan's Southern Region 'ABC' guide. I had two favourite spotting locations – Surbiton, where my grandparents lived, and Elmstead Woods (above), where a like-minded school friend lived. Thus, I could cover routes out of Waterloo, Victoria and Charing Cross, and my 'ABC' is full of West Countries, Battle of Britains, Merchant Navies, Schools, Lord Nelsons and King Arthurs. Years later, I bought the Elmstead Woods totem.

▲ By the time I was thirteen, and at Westminster School in London, my railway enthusiasm had been overshadowed by other teenage interests. However, there was still plenty of train travel. One of the school's sports grounds was at Grove Park, requiring regular journeys from Charing Cross with a special school ticket. Similar tickets for the Underground took me to the boathouse at Putney. Here is St John's, on the Grove Park route, with an SR Schools Class, No. 30908, 'Westminster', passing through in 1957, by which time I had noted it in my 'ABC' book.

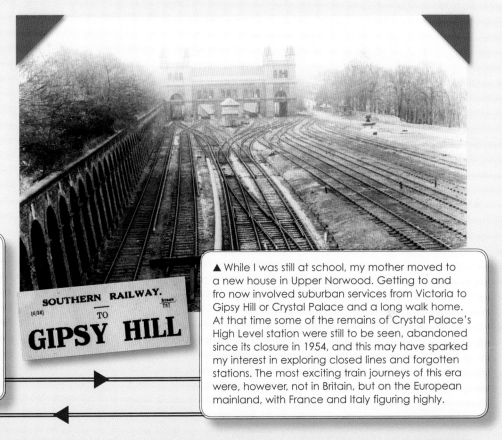

SOUTHERN RAILWAY.
(6/26)   TO
GIPSY HILL

▲ While I was still at school, my mother moved to a new house in Upper Norwood. Getting to and fro now involved suburban services from Victoria to Gipsy Hill or Crystal Palace and a long walk home. At that time some of the remains of Crystal Palace's High Level station were still to be seen, abandoned since its closure in 1954, and this may have sparked my interest in exploring closed lines and forgotten stations. The most exciting train journeys of this era were, however, not in Britain, but on the European mainland, with France and Italy figuring highly.

▼ I was briefly at Keele, in Staffordshire, as a student, and this involved long journeys to Stoke-on-Trent on trains hauled by unfamiliar steam locomotives. It is a pity my trainspotting had completely ceased by then. Later, in the 1970s, I had a long association with Stoke, for work and pleasure, so I came to know the Euston-to-Stoke journey by heart. By then the line was electrified, and the photograph (right) of Stoke station is from that era. Before then, I was a student in Norwich (below), so I came to know well another journey and another London terminus.

Thorpe Station, Norwich

Way Out

Subway to 2,3

▼ In the early 1980s my then wife and I moved to Tackley, in Oxfordshire, with our young family. Remarkably, this village still had a little station, Tackley Halt, and – even more remarkably – expresses from Paddington still stopped there. Short platforms made leaving the train a challenge for the unwary! By this time, I was travelling much more by train, for work and pleasure, and on principle, and my railway enthusiasm, which had never really gone away, was reawakened. There were regular steam specials to watch: below, my daughter Polly waits for one to arrive. Nowadays, of course, Health and Safety would not allow her to sit on the edge of the platform.

▲ After my first marriage ended, I moved back to London, but in 1987 I found by chance and impulsively bought a cottage near Bridport, in Dorset, made from an old GWR carriage. Initially, this was for weekends and for seeing my children, who lived nearby. This meant regular journeys on West Country services from Waterloo to Crewkerne or Dorchester. The former, the Exeter route, was still locomotive-hauled, so that was my preference. Gradually, the cottage – with improvements – became my permanent home.

◄ While I was based in London, I lived for years in a big old flat near Holborn. It was here that I started to write about railways, explore railways and collect railway ephemera. The flat was about a mile from Holborn Underground station and I worked out that over the years I lived there I had walked about a thousand miles between flat and station. I could have walked to Rome! I also used Farringdon, an interesting and useful station when BR's Thameslink services started.

UN TRAIN PEUT EN CACHER UN AUTRE

▲ Another impulsive purchase in the 1980s was a terraced house in Dieppe, starting a pattern of regular visits and holidays. Boat trains from Victoria to Newhaven Marine were still running, just, and rail and boat timetables coincided. So it was an easy journey compared to now. Then, boat trains to and from Paris still ran along the quay in Dieppe to meet the ferry, adding interest to an already lively harbour environment. Sometimes, there were steam specials. I also explored all the local lines, active and derelict.

▲ The first railway book I wrote was *See Britain by Train*, a joint venture between British Rail and The AA – then rather unlikely bedfellows. The research for this involved extensive travelling all over the British network and, as part of the deal, British Rail gave me a First Class All Stations Pass. I had a wonderful time with this, not least because ticket inspectors were always mystified by my having something normally available only to very senior managers. The book was launched with a special railtour on a brand new Class 156 Super Sprinter, suitably badged.

▲ Other books followed, including *Exploring Britain's Lost Railways*, the research for which fuelled my addiction to walking disused railway lines. In 2003 *Branch Line Britain* was published, the first of what is now a long line of highly illustrated railway books. I have spent years tracking down suitable photographs, postcards and bits of railway ephemera for all my books. The publisher is David & Charles, a famous name in railway books. Its offices are in Newton Abbot, so I became very familiar with this famous Devon station, seen here in 1973.

▲ Since 2003 David & Charles has published at least ten of my railway books, so I have, rather unintentionally, become part of the railway scene as one of Britain's best-selling railway writers. I still like railways and everything about them, I travel regularly by train, and I explore all aspects of railway history. I am not addicted to steam, but will always accept a footplate ride if offered. I have done a little bit of driving, and have one regular roster (about twice a year) on the wonderful Beer Heights Light Railway at Pecorama in Devon.

▲ In 2010 my wife and I decided to give up railway-carriage life, so we moved to Weymouth. I sold most of my collection of railway ephemera, old iron signs having no place in a modern townhouse. However, my railway enthusiasm continues unabated, and more books are planned. I still have a vague ambition to travel the entire modern British network. Meanwhile, I have a new station and new routes to get used to, Weymouth turning out to be quite a good starting point for rail journeys across Britain.

Favourite journeys: Weymouth to Portland

My move to Dorset in the late 1980s opened up many new railway possibilities. Sadly, I was too late for the Somerset & Dorset and the Bridport branch, but their routes were there to be explored. A surprising survivor is the line from Bristol to Weymouth, an historic route first planned in the 1840s and finally opened in 1857. Brunel connections, and much else besides, make this a memorable journey across Somerset, Wiltshire and Dorset, and there is the added attraction of ending at the seaside. I have done the

A local, headed by a Class 6100 tank, No. 6157, pauses at Castle Cary in the 1950s. The nameboard invites passengers to change for Somerton and Taunton but ignores Weymouth.

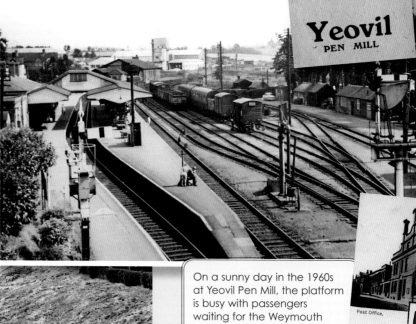

In the 1950s Evershot was a substantial and attractive station, complete with water tower, goods yard and platform planting. It was a long way to the village it served, one of the reasons for its closure. Today nothing remains, but Weymouth trains still pass the site.

G W R
Paddington to
Evershot

On a sunny day in the 1960s at Yeovil Pen Mill, the platform is busy with passengers waiting for the Weymouth train, and the sidings and goods yard are still active. Remarkably, this distinctive station looks much the same today, though the goods wagons have gone. It has semaphore signals and a signal box, so travel to and from Yeovil Pen Mill is a curious railway time warp.

WEYMOUTH STATION c.1860

London and South Western Ry. 787
From ____
TO
Weymouth

journey many times and it never loses its appeal, not least because of the landscape and the places en route – Bath, Bradford-on-Avon, Frome, Castle Cary, Yeovil. It also connects with other main lines.

I must admit that part of this enduring appeal is the presence of request stops such as Chetnole, where you get on by waving to halt the train, and get off by asking the guard to tell the driver to stop. The journey is equally good in both directions, one ending in the splendour of Bristol Temple Meads, the other 200 yards from Weymouth's beach and surrounded by echoes of the town's great railway past.

In the 1950s young enthusiasts wander the platforms at Weymouth, a station that, as a meeting place for Western and Southern region trains, was a spotter's dream. It was a big station, catering for holiday and local traffic. Now, only the platforms on the left survive.

ADMIT ONE TO PLATFORM WEYMOUTH
ON SUNDAY, 12th SEPTEMBER, 1965,
to view LOCOMOTIVE 4472
'Flying Scotsman'
Charge 1/-, allocated to Southern Region
Children's Home
This ticket is issued subject to the Regulations and Conditions contained in the British Commission's Publications and Notices applicable to the Railways

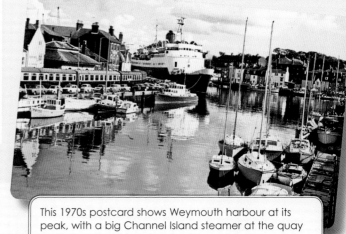

This 1970s postcard shows Weymouth harbour at its peak, with a big Channel Island steamer at the quay and a long boat train leaving Weymouth Quay station for its winding journey through the streets of the town. The trains have gone, although the tracks remain.

Headed by a GWR pannier tank, No. 1368, from the 1930s 1366 Class, a boat train makes its way along the tramway towards Weymouth station in the 1950s. Children stand and watch this daily scene while passengers crowd the windows and the driver keeps a careful watch ahead. The locomotive was a regular on the line through the town until the 1960s.

A very visible part of Weymouth's railway history is the tramway through the streets to the harbour. When I first came here, Channel Island boat trains, led by men with flags, were still crawling to and fro along this, and I was very disappointed when it all stopped in 1987. I did, however, watch the last special to use the line in May 1999. Now living in Weymouth, I am constantly reminded of the tramway and its history, mainly because it is all still there to be seen – the track, the signalling, the crossing gates, the warning signs. This is because it has never been formally closed. Closure is

(2527-F O.P.3.)

GWR _____ 19___

From MORRIS COWLEY (OXON) G.W.36.

SHIPPING GOODS

TO WEYMOUTH QUAY
(FOR JERSEY)

G.W. Rly. _____ Secn. ____

Via _____

Owner and
No. of Wagon | Sheets in or on Wagon

3

Consignee _____

Contents _____

3,000 2/46.

In a classic 1950s Weymouth tramway scene, a GWR pannier tank, No. 7780, takes loaded goods wagons towards the waiting ferries, along a quayside lined with period vehicles and old local barges and fishing boats. The line was originally built for freight traffic and it remained important for supplying the Channel Islands and for the transport of Channel Island produce.

Tank locomotive No. 1368 again, this time in charge of a train of loaded mineral wagons on their way from the quay to Weymouth station in the early 1960s. In the background is the Pavilion Theatre, opened in 1960 to replace the original theatre, destroyed by fire.

Trains on the tramway never failed to attract attention. In this early 1980s scene, railwaymen, now in high visibility vests, lead the boat train away from the quay while the Class 33 diesel crawls behind them.

now likely, and all the remains may be removed, bringing to an end 150 years of very particular local history. Sixty years ago, that is to say within my lifetime, there were many quayside and harbour branches all over Britain. I think this is the last one and, when it goes, the important historical links between railways and shipping will be that much harder to understand.

No trains have used the tramway since 1999, but everything is still in place. Here, near where it branches away from the main line outside Weymouth station, the signals are set at red. In theory, they could go green, to allow a train to go down to the quay. But the track is overgrown and uncared for, and in fact closure is likely.

It is the mid-1980s and the tramway has only a few active years left. The boat train carriages wait at Weymouth Quay station, but there are few passengers.

Until 1965 Weymouth had another branch line, the route to Portland. Inspired largely by local stone traffic and the needs of the Admiralty, the line had a complicated history that ran from the 1820s to 1902, when the complete route to Easton was finally opened. Today, much of the route is visible and accessible, with the section from Ferry Bridge to Weymouth a cycleway. I have walked all of it many times,

This Edwardian postcard, from a painting by AR Quinton, shows the causeway linking Portland and Weymouth. Chesil beach is on the left, and the line of the railway can be seen on the right. Much of the route can still be walked.

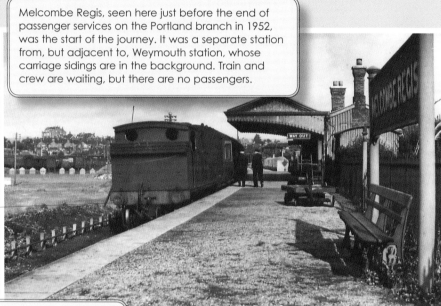

Melcombe Regis, seen here just before the end of passenger services on the Portland branch in 1952, was the start of the journey. It was a separate station from, but adjacent to, Weymouth station, whose carriage sidings are in the background. Train and crew are waiting, but there are no passengers.

The gates are shut, the overgrown track is barred and the signal box is disused. This is Westham soon after closure in 1965. The bridge in the background has gone, along with the buildings, but the platform remains and is the start of the modern cycleway.

The bridge across the Fleet at Smallmouth was finally demolished in 1972. Here, a long special crosses the bridge shortly before closure in 1965. Despite being topped and tailed by locomotives, this six-carriage train had difficulty on the climb towards Easton.

SANDSFOOT CASTLE HALT

and the pleasure never lessens, particularly along the East Weares section below the cliffs, which in landscape terms must have been the most exciting branch line in southern England. The route is littered with echoes of the stone trade, its main raison d'être and one of the things that could justify the line being reopened. I wish I had travelled along it in a train, or at least come to see it in the early 1960s.

This is Portland station in about 1910, at its peak, and the photograph gives an indication of the line's importance. The passenger station is on the left, where the line curves away towards the dockyards, and the extensive sidings on the right are for the stone trade.

(2) 40 SOUTHERN RAILWAY.

FROM WATERLOO TO

PORTLAND (787)

Throughout its life, stone traffic was the backbone of the Portland branch. Here, in May 1958, a train laden with freshly quarried blocks of white Portland stone sets off across the causeway towards Weymouth, hauled, inevitably, by a GWR pannier tank locomotive.

The eastern shore of Portland is rocky and often inaccessible, a place of secret beaches and glorious sea views. Today, the last couple of miles of trackbed leading towards Easton are part of the coast path, and this is really the only way to explore this part of the peninsula. The line climbed steeply below and sometimes through the cliffs before curving inland to the terminus at Easton. It must have been an amazing journey. Nothing remains of Easton station.

An early 1960s railtour, organized by the RCTS, has reached the end of the line at Easton station. As usual, passengers wander all over the place, making the most of a rare trip along a goods-only line. Today, all this has gone.

Favourite journeys: Around the Isle of Wight

In this 1924 postcard Ryde pier is crowded. The pier tramway is still in use, but most people seem happy to stroll in the sun. Hilda writes on the card that she has won a sand competition.

I can trace my passion for the Isle of Wight back to my childhood and day visits in the 1950s with my grandmother. After a quick journey from Surbiton to Portsmouth Harbour station, we would walk down the stairs that took us directly to the quayside and the waiting paddle steamer. The crossing was always the highlight of our day, and we ate our sandwiches on the deck, enjoying the sun and listening to the splash of the paddle wheels. After docking at Ryde Pier Head, we probably walked the half mile along the pier into the town. I'd like to think we took the train for that short journey, but I have no memory of doing so. However,

London and South Western Ry. 787
From WATERLOO TO
MILL HILL
Via PORTSMOUTH & RYDE.

Seen here in British Rail colours in 1968, near the end of her active life, the PS 'Ryde' was one of the stalwarts of the service from Portsmouth. Clyde-built, she was commissioned in 1937.

This delightfully moody photograph, entitled 'Autumn near Wroxhall', captures the atmosphere of the island and its railways. Probably taken in the 1960s, it shows a long train on the embankment near Wroxhall. Much of this section of the Ventnor route is now a footpath.

as I was by then a fully fledged train enthusiast, I must have watched the busy comings and goings of trains along the pier. Sadly, in my Ian Allan Southern Region trainspotter's guide of that era, there are no underlinings in the list of Isle of Wight locomotives. A couple of hours later, the journey was reversed. We never travelled farther afield than Ryde, so the rest of the island remained unknown to me.

My next visit was in 1962, when I was 17 and briefly involved with a girl whose father was then the Bishop of Newport. We made one trip together to the family home in Newport. We must have taken the train from Waterloo to Portsmouth, then the ferry to Ryde and, presumably, the train to Newport, but all I remember about that short visit to the island is the rather unsettling family atmosphere – and my relief at taking the ferry back to Portsmouth in time to catch the last train to London.

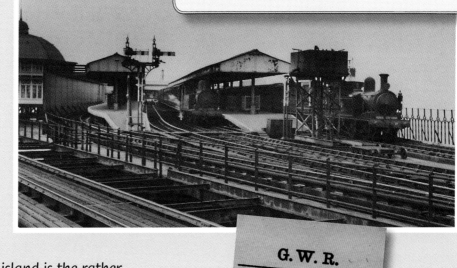

This classic view of Ryde Pier Head station was taken in August 1961, around the time of my brief visit with the Bishop of Newport's daughter. Two trains wait to depart, for Cowes and Ventnor, headed by W26 'Whitwell' and W29 'Alverstone'.

G. W. R.

COWES
(I. of W.)
(VIA BASINGSTOKE)

By 1965 the railway was living on borrowed time, but everything continued as normal. In the early morning at St John's Road, locomotive W28, 'Ashey', marshalls coaching stock for the 06.45 Ryde-to-Ventnor train, in a timeless setting of steam, signal box and gantry.

A few years later I was a regular visitor to the island for family holidays in Seaview, but by then the trains had gone, except for that bizarre, wholly unexpected survivor of the Beeching years, the line from Ryde Pier Head to Shanklin. However, I did see much more of the island, and it began to work its magic. By the 1970s my enthusiasm for all things Victorian had been fully aroused and I realized that the Isle of Wight was, in many ways, a microcosm of Victorian Britain. Monarchy, the military, literature, art, seaside, landscape, architecture – all had tangible Victorian echoes here. The only thing missing was the railway, which had been, until its destruction in the 1960s, the Victorian railway network of Britain in miniature.

I began to look at the remains of the island's railways in earnest in the 1990s, to fill a chapter in the first of my many railway books. Armed with old Ordnance Survey maps and guide books, I spent a wet weekend trying to trace every route of that formerly comprehensive network. Some lines were easily followed, notably those

In September 1952 a solitary passenger leaves the train at Ashey, watched by a small boy and a distant figure with a bicycle. The station, the lamps and the concrete nameboard reflect different eras of ownership. Today Ashey is a halt on the preserved line.

A train waits in Merstone's island platform, but the crossing gates are still against it. Merstone opened in 1875 and later became a junction station for the line to St Lawrence and Ventnor West. Today the junction serves cycle routes, and nothing else remains.

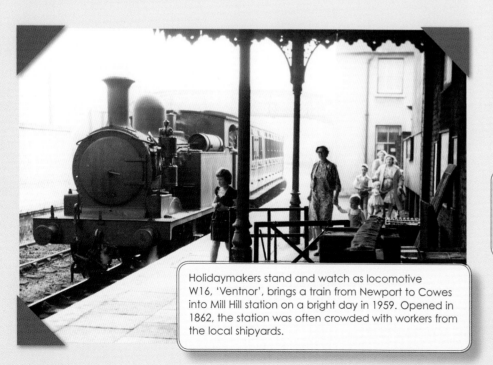

Holidaymakers stand and watch as locomotive W16, 'Ventnor', brings a train from Newport to Cowes into Mill Hill station on a bright day in 1959. Opened in 1862, the station was often crowded with workers from the local shipyards.

(5/33) SOUTHERN RAILWAY. (787 G)
FROM WATERLOO TO
HAVEN STREET
Via PORTSMOUTH.

now back in use as footpaths and bridleways, while others seemed to have vanished into muddy fields and jungle-like woodland. There were station buildings and bridges to be found, and plenty of gates, fence posts and ballast-strewn paths, those lesser markers of former railways. This initial, cursory survey was to be the first of many visits, during which I explored every line in detail, probably exposing myself on occasion to the laws of trespass. Meanwhile, elderly London tube trains trundled to and fro along the Island Line, still meeting the ferries at the end of Ryde pier, and

By 1961 the Isle of Wight's railway network had been significantly pruned, and the surviving lines hardly justified a six-day runabout ticket. However, British Railways continued to encourage tourism to the end.

Six days unlimited travel in the ISLE OF WIGHT with HOLIDAY RUNABOUT TICKETS

Frederick Attrill, seen here at work on his Shell House in East Cowes, was a famous Isle of Wight character until his death in 1926. Tradition has it that he started his shell work after a fight on the beach with Albert Edward, the young Prince of Wales, and a subsequent interview with the Prince's mother in Osborne House.

Opened in 1889, Carisbroke was for years a busy station, thanks to the nearby castle. When buses took that traffic, the station was downgraded to a halt and then closed in 1953, soon after this picture was taken. Nothing remains, and a school now stands on the site.

Isle of Wight Railway.

TO

Brighton

Via South Coast Railway.

An elegant station, Cowes was the first on the island, opening in 1862. Three platforms and plenty of traffic supported for some time a WH Smith bookstall. In this 1950s photograph, the station still has its Southern Railway nameboards. It was demolished after closure, all traces buried under a supermarket car park.

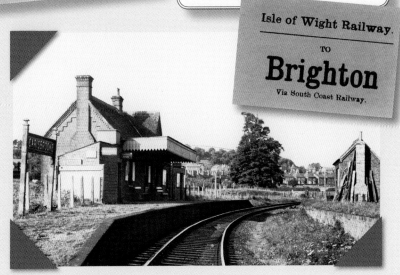

This fine study of an immaculate W15, 'Cowes', resting at Brading in about 1937, shows one of the island's classic 0-4-4 locomotives from the O2 Class, originally an Adams design of 1889. In service until the end of the network, these added greatly to the atmosphere.

The final part of the island's network was the meandering line from Merstone to Ventnor West, opened in 1900 and closed in 1952. Shortly before closure, the driver who has just brought his auto train into the station keeps an eye on the photographer.

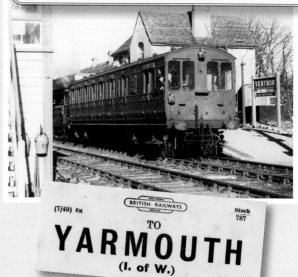

maintaining the close link between rail and sea that was so essential to the Victorians. Not far away, the Isle of Wight Steam Railway was going from strength to strength in its more deliberate re-creation of Victoria's railways.

The Isle of Wight is also a case study in the social impact of railway closures on towns and villages, something never considered at the

The island's main shed was at St John's Road, Ryde, still the depot and workshops for the modern Island Line trains. Here, in 1958, seven of the fleet of Class O2 0-4-4 tank locomotives are packed into a siding, while a single one waits in steam outside the shed.

Trains, headed by W29 'Alverstone' and W17 'Seaview', meet near Newport in the 1960s. The famous viaduct, one of the network's major engineering features, can be seen in the background.

time. Ventnor, once a great resort but now cut off from the mainstream by a hopeless road system (admittedly one of the island's charms), was plunged into depression and decay, and has only recently started to recover. Many villages, formerly kept alive by the railway, faced isolation and lost their amenities and their way of life.

The Isle of Wight is delightfully old fashioned and easily enjoyed, and its railway legacy will always make it one of my favourite places.

By 1968 the tracks at Merstone were overgrown but most of the buildings, including the station and the signal box, still survived. Today, the only railway memory alongside the cycle track is a platform.

In 1882 a short branch was opened from Brading to Bembridge, to serve the harbour. It was closed in 1953, after years of dwindling traffic. This photograph shows Bembridge terminus in 1928.

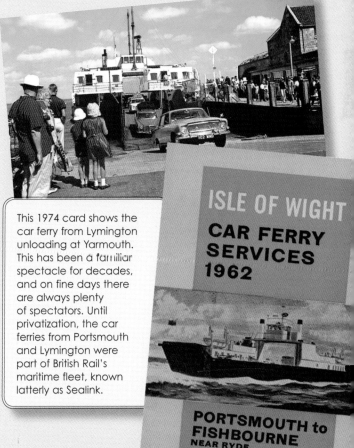

This 1974 card shows the car ferry from Lymington unloading at Yarmouth. This has been a familiar spectacle for decades, and on fine days there are always plenty of spectators. Until privatization, the car ferries from Portsmouth and Lymington were part of British Rail's maritime fleet, known latterly as Sealink.

ISLE OF WIGHT
CAR FERRY SERVICES 1962

PORTSMOUTH to FISHBOURNE NEAR RYDE
LYMINGTON to YARMOUTH

Favourite journeys: The Cambrian Coast

My first visit to West Wales was a holiday in Aberdovey in the early 1950s, and I spent much of the time watching the trains. The Cambrian Coast Line was then very busy, with both passenger and freight traffic along the main line and to and from the many connecting routes. For a small boy staying in a house overlooking the railway, this was heaven. I knew nothing about trains and was too young for the delights of trainspotting, but memories include the sounds – the roaring, clanking and whistling, by day and night – and the regular sight of long, double-headed trains, something little known in my home territory of south London and north Kent. I did not know where these trains were coming from or going to and all I knew about the locomotives was that they

Aberystwyth, the grandest station on the Cambrian Coast Line, was completely rebuilt by the GWR in the 1920s as an important terminus, marked by its clock tower. By the 1970s, traffic was much reduced, though the buildings survived, and do to this day. Vale of Rheidol carriages sit in the foreground.

Opened in 1863, Borth station was designed to encourage holiday traffic to the region and its beaches. In 1958, the station was at the peak of its popularity, though this photograph hardly indicates that. A single Ford sits in the No Parking area and there is no one to be seen. Posters advertise trips to London and local Rover tickets. Now restored after a period of decline, the station houses a local museum.

In the 1960s, Aberdovey was still a substantial station with two platforms and distinctive buildings. On this wet day, it seems tidy but deserted. In the distance the short branch to the harbour swings away. Today, there is just one platform.

CAMBRIAN RAILWAYS. TO Aberdovey

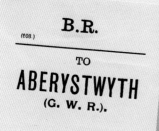

B.R.
(E08.)

TO
ABERYSTWYTH
(G. W. R.).

Running light on a sunny day in the 1950s, a GWR locomotive enters Barmouth Junction station – a scene full of period detail. The nameboard tells passengers to change here for Dolgellau, Bala, Llangollen and Chester, a route that closed in the 1960s. Now, there is no junction and the station, such as it is, has been renamed Morfa Mawddach.

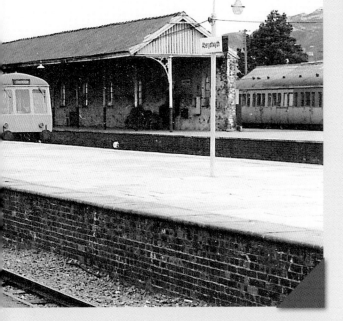

In the 1960s, Tywyn still had a goods shed, an active goods yard and a signal box. Today, practically everything has gone and the station, whose two platforms and footbridge are visible in the distance, is much reduced.

CAMBRIAN RAILWAYS.
TO
BARMOUTH

were green or black. There was just an ever-changing panorama in front of me, with trains passing back and forth against a backdrop of sand dunes, sea and sky. As ever, my memories are of continuously sunny days. Since then, I have always loved the sight of trains against the glittering sea, and most of my favourite train journeys in Britain are either by the sea, or include the seascape.

On that first visit I don't think we went much farther than the beach or the town, and certainly there were no train journeys. I realize now that I could have been taken to visit the Talyllyn Railway at the very start of its long road to preservation, but it did not happen. A second visit to Wales when I was about eleven did include a trip on the Snowdon Mountain Railway, but by then I was well into my trainspotting days. All other travel was by car

This postcard view of Barmouth, its beach and harbour, and the elevated route of the railway through the town, dates from about 1964. There is even a long steam train setting off towards the great viaduct across the estuary en route to Aberystwyth or Chester. Postcards more commonly show views of the viaduct and the estuary, the long wooden structure having been a major feature since 1867.

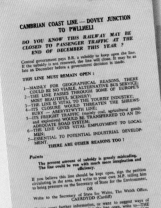

This bilingual leaflet is a legacy of the battle to keep the Cambrian Coast route open in the 1960s and 1970s. It was believed that the loss of the government subsidy that maintained the line would bring closure to the section from Dovey Junction to Pwllheli.

as my mother, never a train fan, always did her best to avoid railway journeys. After that visit, I was not to return to Wales for many years.

In the 1970s, regular visits to West and North Wales started again, but these had little to do with trains. Trips to Bangor, for work, and to Portmeirion, for pleasure, were quite common at that time, and the latter generally included trips on the Ffestiniog Railway and walks among the derelict slate lines around Blaenau and along the long-forgotten Welsh Highland route. It was impossible then to imagine that trains could ever run again along that spectacular route to Caernarfon.

It was not until the 1980s that I actually travelled the full length of the surviving Cambrian Coast Line, one of the many research journeys I made for my first railway book. By then everything I remembered had gone, including steam, freight trains, double tracks, sidings and shunting, and the constant movement of traffic. The

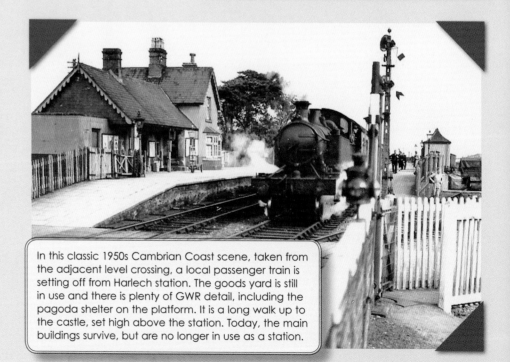

Coastal railways often suffer from problems caused by erosion, particularly during winter storms, so constant maintenance is necessary. Here, in the 1960s, an engineering team is at work protecting the track by building up piles of rock along the foreshore by Llanaber station. During the repairs, which required the use of a large travelling crane, the single-track line would have been closed to normal services.

In this classic 1950s Cambrian Coast scene, taken from the adjacent level crossing, a local passenger train is setting off from Harlech station. The goods yard is still in use and there is plenty of GWR detail, including the pagoda shelter on the platform. It is a long walk up to the castle, set high above the station. Today, the main buildings survive, but are no longer in use as a station.

majority of the connecting lines had been closed in the 1960s, and what remained was a shadow of past glories, with most services operated by diesel railcars. At that time of post-Beeching closures, the whole Cambrian Coast route had been under threat, inconceivable though that seems today. The journey, from Aberystwyth to Pwllheli, was a sad experience of run-down services, slow trains and semi-abandoned stations. Despite this, the route was still high on my list of Britain's great railway journeys, and unique in its mixture of landscape and seaside. Indeed, the Cambrian Coast Line is still Britain's greatest seaside journey, and an exciting voyage through an incomparable landscape that is filled with echoes of dramatic history.

Over the next few years there were more trips along the line, but usually at the northern end, in the course of holidays and in the pursuit of lost lines, which I was tracking down, exploring and photographing for a new series of railway

A woman and her dog are the only passengers waiting at Minffordd station as the DMU rattles into the single platform on a rather gloomy day in the 1960s. There is not even a shelter, yet this was quite an important station, serving Portmeirion village and the adjacent station on the Ffestiniog Railway. Indeed, the station nameboard instructs passengers to change here for the Ffestiniog.

Another woman and her dog walk past Llandanwg station, a typical Cambrian Line halt set in marshland and coastal pastures and without direct road access. Despite this, and its very basic nature, the station is currently used by about 5,000 people per year.

As this 1905 card suggests, Harlech Castle dominates its town and the surrounding hills, which drop down sharply towards the sea. The station is far below and to the left, almost at sea level, and passengers prepared to stretch their necks can look up towards the castle.

books. There were also a couple of trips to Aberystwyth, to explore the lost line to the south of that town. Throughout this period, things began to show signs of improvement. Stations and infrastructure were being tidied up and repaired, the Barmouth Viaduct was fully restored, and new trains began to appear as the chaos created by the process of privatization started to diminish. A surprising number of minor stations and unmanned halts had survived, and some of these took on a new lease of life once they had escaped the closure threats of the 1990s, adding to the line's appeal. Larger station buildings had also survived, having been converted in some cases into private houses. The qualities of the route and its landscape and history were heavily promoted, and steam-hauled and other specials made regular appearances. At last, it was possible to enjoy the sight and sound of a long, steam-hauled excursion train travelling along the Cambrian Coast, something that almost took me back to my distant childhood and the memories of that holiday when a small boy's lifelong fascination with trains began.

This charming Edwardian view of Talsarnau station features passengers and staff carefully posed by the photographer, who is standing on the track. The woman with her splendid pram, her child and their dog makes a good focal point. Today, the station buildings are a private house.

The flags are flying at Abererch Halt, perhaps for the Queen's coronation in 1953. There are some fine flowers and a typically low platform, hence the passenger steps. A camping coach with a clerestory roof can be seen in a siding beyond the level crossing, whose gate-keeper lived in the cottage. Attempts to close this and other minor Cambrian Line halts in 1971 and the 1990s were thwarted by public pressure.

Running tender first, an old GWR 0-6-0 goods locomotive draws a long line of assorted plank wagons slowly through Porthmadog station, probably in the 1920s. Advertising signs are displayed on the side of the station building, and the large water tower can be seen in the background.

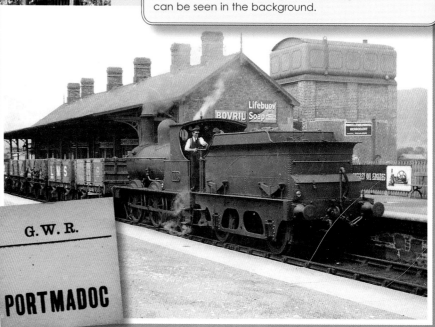

G.W.R. PORTMADOC

This scene of dereliction is Afon Wen station and junction, soon after the closure of the line northwards to Caernarfon and Bangor in 1964. In this remote spot, the track has been torn up, the signal box is a ruin and the water towers are on their last legs, yet the trains are still running. Today, the station is long gone but the main building survives as a private house. Everything else in the picture has vanished.

In the late 1950s an old GWR Class 2251 0-6-0 goods locomotive, No. 2233, brings a mixed freight slowly into Criccieth station. Then, there were two platforms and direct services to London Euston via Bangor and to London Paddington via Shrewsbury. Now, it is a one-platform, unstaffed halt, and here too the main building has been converted into a private house.

Taff Vale Railway

MOUNTAIN ASH

TO

PWLLLELI

This rural scene by the famous postcard artist AR Quinton shows the boyhood home of David Lloyd George, whose early years were spent in this old stone house at Llanystumdwy, near Criccieth. Today, it houses a museum dedicated to the life of this famous British Prime Minister.

Although Pwllheli is the end of the Cambrian Coast Line, it was possible at one time to continue westwards along the coast to Llanbedrog by horse-drawn tram. This 3ft gauge line was opened in 1894, extended in 1897 and closed in 1927 after a storm washed away much of the track. The tramway, shown here in the early 1920s, was built by Solomon Andrews, a local developer keen to expand the holiday trade.

Favourite journeys: Oxford to Hereford

My railway connections with Oxford date from about 1979 when we moved to Tackley, a small village near Woodstock, hitherto unknown to me. I was delighted to find it had a station, with two short platforms decorated with the old GWR Tackley Halt nameboards. Sadly, these were soon replaced by something in plastic, though the word Halt survived the transition. I used the station as often as possible, having discovered that big trains bound for Birmingham and London sometimes stopped here.

Oxford's railway station has changed a number of times since it was first opened in the 1840s. By the 1950s, this late Victorian version was looking past its best, and complete redevelopment was on the way.

Oxford must have generated thousands of postcards, but this view of Brasenose College and the Radcliffe Camera, with its gowned scholar and straw-hatted tourist, is a classic. It was posted in December 1904 by a young man starting a courtship.

Throughout its long life, the route from Oxford to Worcester and Hereford has witnessed many great trains and famous locomotives. By the 1990s the line was being operated as part of the InterCity network, and HST 125s were in charge, suitably liveried. This photograph, showing a summer scene north of Oxford, was taken towards the end of the British Rail era, and soon everything was to change.

G.W.R.

OXFORD

Adlestrop station opened in 1853 and closed in 1966. This 1950s view shows the neatly planted, tidy platforms and the goods shed of a typical country station, made exceptional by Edward Thomas's poem 'Adlestrop', about an express that '... drew up there Unwontedly'. Here, a local headed by a Class 4300 2-6-0 locomotive, No. 6349, makes a scheduled stop.

G.W.R.
Adlestrop

DISCOVER THE BEAUTY OF THE Cotswolds and Malverns on Britain's Scenic Railway

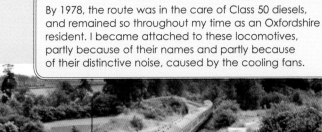

However, most of my travelling at that time was from Oxford. For a while, I was a regular commuter to London, the tedium of which was relieved by regular journeys on the Class 50-hauled trains on the Hereford route, the start of a long attachment to these particular locomotives with their resonant warship names. For various reasons, including curiosity, I began to travel in the other direction, and was soon

By 1978, the route was in the care of Class 50 diesels, and remained so throughout my time as an Oxfordshire resident. I became attached to these locomotives, partly because of their names and partly because of their distinctive noise, caused by the cooling fans.

Kingham's nameboard invites passengers to change for the Chipping Norton, Bourton-on-the-Water and Cheltenham lines. In September 1961, when Kingham was still a railway crossroads, a GWR Modified Hall, No. 7903, 'Foremarke Hall', has paused to take on water.

This early 20th-century view shows Evesham station on a quiet day. A few passengers are waiting, luggage is piled up on the platform, and the shunting horse is dozing in the sun by the signal box. The goods yard is full, reflecting the busy junction with the Birmingham-to-Ashchurch line.

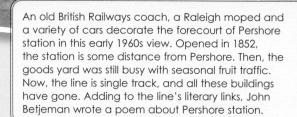

addicted to the delights of what British Rail called the Cotswolds and Malverns Line. As ever, landscape and history gave the journey an enduring appeal, made distinctive by the wonderful colour of the Cotswold stone and the ever-changing backdrop of hills. The line links a long sequence of famous places, including Moreton-in-Marsh, Evesham, Worcester, Malvern, Ledbury and Hereford, all known to me for various reasons but discovered anew from the train.

I also pieced together the line's history, a complex one that included the infamous Oxford, Worcester & Wolverhampton Railway, popularly known as the Old Worse & Worse. There is a Brunel link in Charlbury station, a delightful reminder of his enthusiasm for the Italianate style.

An old British Railways coach, a Raleigh moped and a variety of cars decorate the forecourt of Pershore station in this early 1960s view. Opened in 1852, the station is some distance from Pershore. Then, the goods yard was still busy with seasonal fruit traffic. Now, the line is single track, and all these buildings have gone. Adding to the line's literary links, John Betjeman wrote a poem about Pershore station.

G.W.R.

WORCESTER

(Foregate Street)

The line connects both Worcester's stations, Shrub Hill and Foregate Street. This is the latter, photographed during the early 1960s, as GWR Castle Class No. 5012, 'Berry Pomeroy Castle', paused there. The normally busy station, built on a curving, elevated site, seems unusually deserted. The raised signal box survives, but is no longer in use.

The line's many lost connections added excitement and made me regret, as ever, that I hadn't explored them when they were open. At its peak, the line was the backbone of a thriving GWR network, with railway crossroads at Kingham, Honeybourne and Evesham, and plenty of other junctions along the way. Some of these routes I have since explored as lost lines, following the dotted line on the

Residence of the late Madame Jenny Lind Goldschmidt, Wynd's Point near Malvern.

Great Malvern station is a famously decorative building, designed by EW Elmslie in 1862 for the Worcester & Hereford Railway, later the GWR. The style is French Gothic, with rich detailing inside and out, including foliate iron capitals on the platforms. The clock was removed in the 1960s, for no good reason.

This card, posted in 1907, shows the last home of Jenny Lind, the singer known as 'the Swedish nightingale'. After an adventurous life, she moved to Wynd's Point, near the Malvern hills, with her husband and children, and died here in 1887, having given her last concert four years earlier.

Assorted spectators, including the inevitable small boy, stand and watch while a rather dirty and decrepit GWR locomotive pours out a fearful cloud of smoke as it struggles to haul a long load of mineral wagons up a slight incline near Malvern in 1960.

By the early 1960s, diesels were becoming a regular sight on the line. In 1963 this Manchester-built Hymek, D7076, seen here near Ledbury, was brand new, and smartly finished in the green livery of that era. Withdrawn after only ten years' service, the locomotive was used for research purposes until rescued for preservation in 1983.

A Class 7200 heavy duty freight 2-8-2 tank locomotive, No. 7251, hauls its line of open wagons onto the single-track section near Colwall during the summer of 1960. Freight traffic was then still important on the route, thanks to the many connections with other lines.

Staff and passengers pass the time of day as a mixed freight passes slowly through Colwall station in the early 1960s. Nothing of this survives, and the station has just a single track and one platform.

Ordnance Survey map to see what remains to be found. Enjoyable though that process is, however, the real thing must have been better – as, I hope, the photographs I have chosen indicate.

The past is always alluring, but it must not be allowed to diminish the present. The Oxford-to-Hereford route is still a great railway journey, offering a particular vision of English history that is 'best seen when you travel by train' – as British Rail described it in the late 1980s, when they were promoting this, and many other routes around the country, as Britain's Scenic Railway.

Hereford station, originally one of two in the town and therefore known as Barr's Court, was opened in 1855. It is a grand brick building in a decorative Tudor style deemed suitable for the city and was, until the 1960s, a busy place and the meeting point for several lines. Today, things are simpler. TW Penson's ambitious building still stands, but is no longer in railway use.

In 1964 an immaculate GWR Castle Class locomotive hauls an equally gleaming set of carriages out of Ledbury Tunnel. The train was a special organized by the Oxford University Railway Society, and the members are making the most of the open windows.

G. W. R.

HEREFORD

Hereford, High Town.

This Edwardian card captures the flavour of Hereford at that time. Sent by a little girl to a friend in Southend-on-Sea, it describes her excitement at seeing the *Daily Mail*'s Flying Machine, something linked perhaps to the famous London-to-Manchester Air Race of 1910.

Favourite journeys: Around Norwich

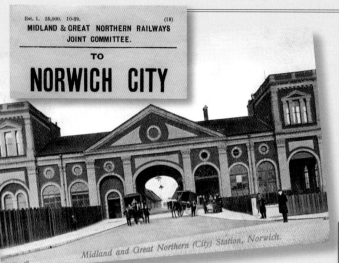

Est. I. 25,000. 10-29. (18)
MIDLAND & GREAT NORTHERN RAILWAYS
JOINT COMMITTEE.

TO

NORWICH CITY

Midland and Great Northern (City) Station, Norwich.

From 1969 to 1972 I was a student at the University of East Anglia and I made the most of this opportunity to get to know Norwich and Norfolk. My father grew up in Suffolk, so East Anglia was not unfamiliar territory. At this time, railways were not at the top of my agenda, but I did explore what remained in use of Norfolk's once comprehensive network. With part of my life still London based, I also developed an intimate familiarity with the main line between Norwich and Liverpool Street. But, looking back, I realize I could have

Norwich City is not just a football club; it was also a railway station, the terminus of the M&GNJR's route into the city. This Edwardian card shows an imposing, if architecturally unusual, structure, the company's public face in a city dominated by other, better-known railways. Today nothing remains, and few people even know of Norwich's other stations.

Several companies were taken into the M&GNJR when it was formed in 1893. An important one was the Lynn & Fakenham Railway, and it was they who built Whitwell & Reepham station, a typical low-cost, cottage-style structure. Here it is in the late 1990s, when little seemed to have happened since the last train passed through some fifteen years earlier. It has now been fully restored as a private house and is the headquarters of a railway preservation society.

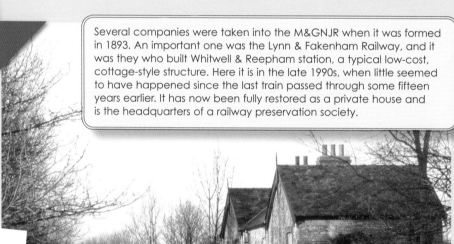

Drayton station, seen here in about 1900 with a mixed freight passing through, served a village later absorbed into the suburbs of Norwich. The M&GNJR had been set up by the Midland Railway and the Great Northern Railway to give those big companies access to East Anglia, particularly for freight traffic. The cross-country route had many connections with other lines, all of which were seen as advantageous.

An elegant skew bridge, beautifully built from red brick, spans an overgrown trackbed – a remote reminder of a long-lost railway. Such structures can be seen all over the M&GN network, surviving because there has been no reason to pull them down.

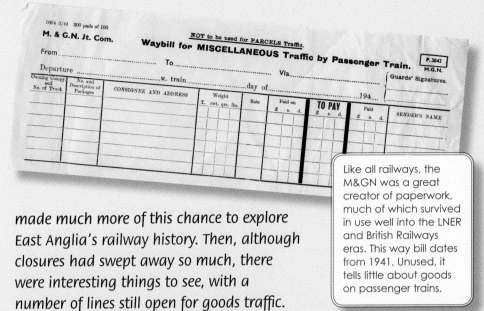

Like all railways, the M&GN was a great creator of paperwork, much of which survived in use well into the LNER and British Railways eras. This way bill dates from 1941. Unused, it tells little about goods on passenger trains.

made much more of this chance to explore East Anglia's railway history. Then, although closures had swept away so much, there were interesting things to see, with a number of lines still open for goods traffic.

Later, I tried to make up for these lost opportunities by steadily exploring the whole of the Norfolk network, and in doing so I became intrigued by the story of that eccentric and ponderously named company, the Midland & Great Northern Joint Railway (more simply, the M&GN). Determinedly independent, it had successfully served many corners and remote parts of a largely rural region and operated a complicated timetable over mostly single-track routes. The closure of most of the M&GN in 1959 was a great

The centre of the network, a railway crossroads and the site of the railway's locomotive works, Melton Constable turned from a little village into a large railway town. The Lynn & Fakenham started it, and the M&GN greatly expanded it.

The glory days of Melton Constable are long since gone, and it has now reverted to being a small country town. Very little remains to illustrate its busy railway past other than this water tower, photographed in the 1990s.

When railways disappear, they leave traces scattered all over the place. Farmers have always made use of retired goods vehicles and in Norfolk, thanks in part to the decline in freight traffic, there was a ready supply of these until the late 1950s. It would be nice to think that this van body had run along M&GN metals.

After the closures of 1959, only the M&GN line from Cromer to Melton Constable via Sheringham remained open, and DMUs were introduced to save costs. This is Holt on a wet day in 1965, shortly before this section closed as well.

After 1965, Sheringham became the terminus of the former Great Eastern Railway's line from Norwich. However, the original station, at the other side of a busy level crossing, was closed, and a new basic, single-platform station, seen here in the late 1960s, was opened and the crossing removed. The old station was taken over by the preserved North Norfolk Railway (the Poppy Line), as the starting point for their reopened route to Holt. In 2011, the level crossing was reinstated, once more connecting Sheringham's old station, and the Poppy Line, to the national network.

loss, making much of Norfolk inaccessible and isolating those without cars. I started my explorations in the late 1980s and over the next twenty years followed most of the M&GN network through the fields into which it had often vanished. While large sections had been lost completely, there was plenty to be enjoyed by the dedicated explorer, including bridges, stations and other parts of the built infrastructure. More apparent was the impact of the railway on the landscape – the cuttings and embankments that still crossed the fields, visible ghosts of a long-lost network. Small sections survive in use, with National

The North Norfolk Railway is a premier preserved railway, operating between Sheringham and Holt. Its fleet includes steam and diesel locomotives, including this fine Class 31.

In the 1920s, a 4-4-2 tank locomotive built at Melton Constable in 1909 pulls away from the M&GN's Cromer Beach station, whose central position boosted the resort's popularity. The present-day line from Sheringham to Norwich, now marketed as the Bittern Line, still uses Cromer Beach station, though the original elegant, timber-framed building, erected in 1887, is now a restaurant.

Cromer became a popular resort in the late Victorian period, and was served by two railway companies. Writing this card in 1912 to a friend in Kent, Norma found it 'a very pretty and quiet place'.

G. E. R.
Cromer

Both the M&GN and the GER had stations at North Walsham. The GER's 1896 signal box, a typical timber design with a projecting bay window, was in use when photographed in the 1990s but became redundant in 2000 and was later demolished. Of the stations, only the former GER station survives, albeit much reduced. When there were two stations, this one was called North Walsham Main, the other North Walsham Town.

Rail services between Cromer and Sheringham and the preserved North Norfolk Railway operating between Holt and Sheringham. The mix of exploring lost routes and travelling on lines that are active – on the national network or preserved – is appealing.

So my journey is a circuit from Norwich to Norwich, visiting obscure corners of the Midland & Great Northern Joint Railway and taking in the former Great Eastern Railway route from Sheringham to Norwich via Cromer.

Worstead, a village whose name is an echo of East Anglian textile wealth in the Middle Ages, had a substantial station when this photograph was taken in about 1910. The driver of the Cromer-bound train is leaning out to take the single-line token.

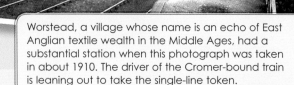

Wroxham is traditionally the heart of the Norfolk Broads, as this 1960s card suggests. The station was until 1982 the junction for the line to Aylsham, something I could have explored as a student. Today, the Bure Valley narrow gauge line uses the trackbed.

WROXHAM BRIDGE, NORFOLK BROADS

Today, Worstead's main station building and its canopy survive, one of a few to escape destruction. There is only one track and the other platform was a bit overgrown in 2002, when this two-car Class 150 DMU paused on its way from Norwich to Sheringham.

G. E. R.

From

TO

SALHOUSE

Salhouse, seen here in the 1960s, is another example of a Great Eastern country station that can still be enjoyed today. The surrounding area has been much developed since the photograph was taken, bringing more people onto the train, with about 6,000 passengers a year using the station and its small car park.

NORWICH, CASTLE & CATTLE MARKET.

This card, showing Norwich Castle and the cattle market, was posted in Ohio in September 1911. The transport of livestock was a major railway activity at that time, with the M&GN a lifeline for rural farmers.

Norwich's grand, French-style GER terminus of 1886 is now the city's only station, so no longer carries the name Thorpe. Now restored, the station is a fine start and end point for East Anglian railway journeys. Here, in 1979, a DMU crosses the junction outside the station where the tracks from London, on the right, meet those from Lowestoft, Yarmouth and Sheringham.

Favourite journeys: Around Whitby

Middlesbrough still has a magnificent Gothic station in coloured brick, but the 1877 building looked much more impressive when this Edwardian card was posted. Still present then is the great iron train shed, removed after bomb damage during World War II.

There are certain places that get under your skin, and for me Whitby is quite high on that list. My first visit was in the mid-1960s, when a friend and I were touring the North of England looking for things to put in an antiques shop that was briefly part of my life, and I still remember the impact of the town and its harbour, the shops selling jet, and the walk up to the ruins of the abbey. It was almost like the start of a love affair. I have since been back many times, and it has always felt the same, in rain or sun.

In those distant 1960s days I wasn't thinking much about railways, so

DISCOVER THE Esk Valley on Britain's Scenic Railway

The modern journey to Whitby involves a reversal at Battersby, today a rather bleak and isolated station. In this busy scene photographed in 1957, an LNER Class V3 tank, No. 67646, is running round its train.

L. & N. E. R.

From Middlesbrough

Saltburn was an early railway resort, created during the 1860s, and the station building, with its classical porte cochère in coloured brick, dates from 1862. At the end of a branch, which also served the Zetland Hotel, the station, along with its line, is a surprising survivor.

I missed everything I could then have seen and enjoyed. My first visit to Whitby by train was in the 1980s, and the slow journey from Middlesbrough in an old DMU was a revelation. Everything was exciting: the landscape, the views, the old stone stations – some still with their clocks set into the wall, the leisurely exchange of single-line tokens while geese squawked in the adjacent field and, above all, the end-of-the-line feeling combined with a strong sense of history. Most memorable was the final approach to Whitby along the Esk

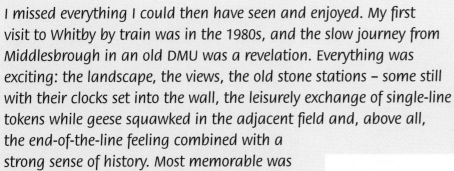

Another resort from the 1860s, with a station to match, Redcar also became an important industrial centre. This 1930s card suggests that holidays were still important then.

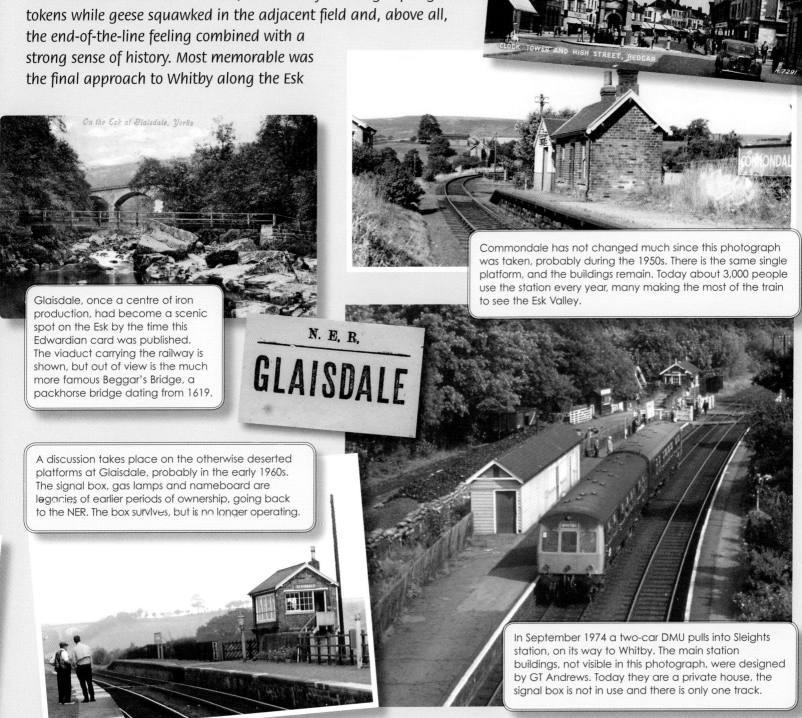

Commondale has not changed much since this photograph was taken, probably during the 1950s. There is the same single platform, and the buildings remain. Today about 3,000 people use the station every year, many making the most of the train to see the Esk Valley.

Glaisdale, once a centre of iron production, had become a scenic spot on the Esk by the time this Edwardian card was published. The viaduct carrying the railway is shown, but out of view is the much more famous Beggar's Bridge, a packhorse bridge dating from 1619.

N. E. R.
GLAISDALE

A discussion takes place on the otherwise deserted platforms at Glaisdale, probably in the early 1960s. The signal box, gas lamps and nameboard are legacies of earlier periods of ownership, going back to the NER. The box survives, but is no longer operating.

In September 1974 a two-car DMU pulls into Sleights station, on its way to Whitby. The main station buildings, not visible in this photograph, were designed by GT Andrews. Today they are a private house, the signal box is not in use and there is only one track.

LONDON & NORTH EASTERN RAILWAY.

From

Grosmont

WHITBY FROM SPION KOP

Whitby is set among hills, offering great views over the harbour. This 1920s card shows the view from Spion Kop, looking out towards the lift bridge and the harbour. It was this prospect that inspired Bram Stoker, while holidaying here in the 1890s, to write *Dracula*.

Grosmont station dates back to the 1830s, as part of the Whitby & Pickering Railway. Extensively developed by later owners, it is now the meeting point for the North Yorkshire Moors Railway and the Esk Valley Line. This 1958 view shows a York-to-Whitby service leaving Grosmont, behind an LMS Class 4 tank, No. 42085.

In July 1953 an LNER Class B1, No. 61053, is about to depart for York from Whitby Town. Ahead is the stone engine shed, dating back to 1847, the year this once-great station, designed by GT Andrews and inspired by George Hudson, the 'Railway King', was opened.

Two smart and cheerful ladies pose on the platform at Whitby in about 1920, prior to a shopping trip to York. Long established as a port, Whitby developed a new life as a resort from the 1850s and the railway was the driving force. From then on, it was a popular place for holidays and excursions, particularly with British Railways.

BRITISH RAILWAYS

EXCURSION

TO

WHITBY
(TOWN)

Whit Monday 7th June 1954

46

The extensive carriage sidings outside Whitby Town station, built over a riverside area known as Bog Hall, reflected the railway's busy holiday traffic. In this 1958 view, an LMS Class 4 tank, No. 42083, is busy shunting empty stock.

L.N.E.R.
LUGGAGE
From WHITBY
To
via TEBAY
and L.M.S.
S.S. 5219 M 9793
TE

and into the station, an old NER tiled route map on the platform reminding me of its much grander days. Since then, I have done the journey several times, and it has never disappointed.

I came to realize that today's Esk Valley Line is the surviving part of a much larger local network, with at least three ways of approaching Whitby. By then, I was well into my enthusiasm for lost railways, and I spent time tracing and exploring the old

An incline up Prospect Hill linked Whitby's two stations, Town and West Cliff. In this 1958 view a DMU bound for Scarborough grinds up the hill. After stopping at West Cliff, this train will reverse and set off southwards, crossing Larpool Viaduct, seen in the background.

In another 1950s view, Class 4 tank No. 42085 draws into Whitby's West Cliff station. The station, opened in 1883, was set high above the town for trains on the coastal route. It closed finally in 1961, but the buildings survive in a housing development.

The coastal route from Whitby West Cliff to Redcar and Middlesbrough was a famously spectacular journey. The route included several tunnels and two dramatic iron viaducts. This is Sandsend in the 1950s, with a Middlesbrough train running into the station. The line closed in 1958.

Several stations along the coastal route enjoyed glorious views. This is Kettleness in about 1960, a big station built to serve a small community. The tracks have gone and the buildings look empty.

network, notably the coast route from Redcar to Whitby and onwards to Scarborough, surely one of England's loveliest train journeys. I also went inland, to explore the old Rosedale mineral lines, which offer some exhilarating railway walking. Much later, I travelled for the first time on the North Yorkshire Moors preserved line, a magnificent trip to Grosmont, before their steam trains were allowed to continue over Network Rail's tracks into Whitby.

I have brought together here a journey of past and present, with a look at the existing Whitby line, what used to be and what remains.

This photograph, taken in the 1990s, shows the magnificent and remote setting that Kettleness station enjoyed, as well as the scale and elegant symmetry of the buildings. At that time it was a private house; now it has been converted for use as an activity centre.

In the 1990s the coastal route could be followed and explored with some difficulty, as stretches had become overgrown. The effect though was often picturesque, as in this view near Kettleness where only the bridge reveals the existence of the trackbed.

NORTH EASTERN RAILWAY,
from WHITBY
Hinderwell (FOR RUNS-
WICK BAY)

A highpoint of any journey must have been the crossing of the Staithes Viaduct. This iron structure, 700ft long, was built in 1875 but not opened until 1883, with the rest of the line. It was exposed to high winds, and trains had to observe a 20mph speed limit. Gales stopped all traffic completely. Both this and Sandsend were demolished in 1960, but the northern parapet survives, along with the station, at the southern end.

A famously attractive village built along the steep banks of Roxby Beck, Staithes had a large fishing fleet that used its sheltered harbour. It was also a magnet for artists in the 1920s and 1930s. This 1950s view shows the viaduct in the background.

Favourite journeys: The Far North

In the late 1980s, armed with a First Class All Stations BR staff pass, I spent a few months travelling on trains all over Britain while researching a book. The highlight of this rather extraordinary period was a week exploring every significant line in Scotland. With the exception of Mallaig and Oban, everything was new to me. It was the confirmation of a long-held belief that, when it comes to enjoying landscape, nothing beats the train window. All railway routes in Scotland have something special, but the revelation to me was the sheer spectacle and excitement of what is now known as the Far North Line.

British Rail worked hard at promoting the holiday potential of its Scottish routes, with a range of special fares linked to sleepers and motorail. Typical is this 1978 brochure.

DISCOVER SCOTLAND BY TRAIN 1978

Inter-City

This early 20th-century postcard offers a romantic vision of Beauly in afternoon sunlight. It is not quite the view from the train, but deer are often to be seen along the route, particularly on the long inland stretch to the north of Helmsdale.

Afternoon Sunshine Beauly. E. Longstaffe

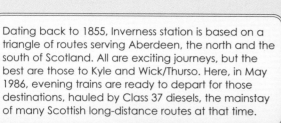

The Highland Railway Company.
LUGGAGE.
DINGWALL

Dating back to 1855, Inverness station is based on a triangle of routes serving Aberdeen, the north and the south of Scotland. All are exciting journeys, but the best are those to Kyle and Wick/Thurso. Here, in May 1986, evening trains are ready to depart for those destinations, hauled by Class 37 diesels, the mainstay of many Scottish long-distance routes at that time.

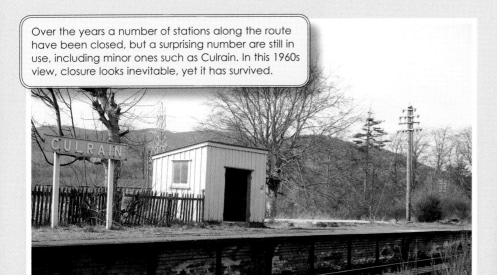

Over the years a number of stations along the route have been closed, but a surprising number are still in use, including minor ones such as Culrain. In this 1960s view, closure looks inevitable, yet it has survived.

In the Edwardian era Invergordon was a busy station serving the naval base there. Later, the whisky trade kept the sidings full and, when I first travelled the line, the oil boom had brought life back to Cromarty Firth.

Land cruises and other special tour trains ran regularly over northern Scottish routes from the 1980s. Here, in May 1992, a pair of Class 37 diesels in contrasting liveries haul an InterCity land cruise across the bridge over the Oykel at Invershin, in a classic setting.

Dunrobin Castle, depicted here with coat of arms and tartan on an Edwardian postcard, is the Victorian seat of the Dukes of Sutherland, and one of the many sights along the route.

The Duke of Sutherland, as a major backer of the line, had his own station at Dunrobin. The timber-framed building is still in use as a request stop when the castle is open to the general public, but the siding, for the Duke's private train, has gone.

When the Sutherland Railway ran out of money at Golspie, the Duke of Sutherland extended the line to Helmsdale. He ran it for a year until it came under the control of the Highland Railway in 1871. In 1895 the Duke took delivery of 'Dunrobin', and two private saloons for his own use. In 1965 they went to Canada, but are now back.

Brora was opened in June 1871, quite a substantial station to serve a typically small community. Here, in the 1950s, various station staff have taken a break to watch the passage of a mixed freight, headed by a Class 5MT, No. 45098. Today, Brora still has its original buildings and sees over 5,000 passengers a year.

Great North of Scotland Railway.

LUGGAGE

BRORA

FROM ABERDEEN.

I remember arriving at Inverness, after a long day's travel, to catch the 17.00 for Wick and Thurso, and being astonished that we had another four and a half hours on the train. Luckily, we had brought a picnic and found a seat with a table. It was a sunny summer evening, and the hours passed pleasurably as the landscape unrolled with its breathtaking diversity of colour and wilderness. The sense of emptiness was underlined by the sequence of ever more remote stations serving tiny communities, yet people got on and off. It was hard to believe that such a line had ever been built, let alone survived the cuts of the 1960s. I knew, of course, the history: the importance of the Duke of Sutherland in its construction, its role as the lifeline to Scapa Flow in two world wars, and its enduring importance as a community railway. On this trip, it was still a large, locomotive-hauled train, so I was able to witness the complicated juggling that took place at Georgemas Junction.

In this 1960s view, with patches of snow on the ground, Forsinard had clearly seen better days. The crossing gates are tatty, the station building looks unloved, and there is a range of old notices, but the line is still busy and the signal box in use.

On a sunny day in June 1987, the train from Inverness draws into Georgemas Junction, headed by one of the ubiquitous Class 37, in this case No. 37420. The post van waits, door open to receive the mailbags. Here, the train will split, the front half continuing to Wick, while a matching locomotive, waiting at the junction, will take the other half to Thurso. This complicated procedure, a feature of the line from its opening, was repeated several times a day until locomotives were finally withdrawn from the route in the early 1990s.

In this 1970s view of Wick, the train from Inverness has arrived and the passengers have scattered, leaving one man mooching along the platform. Posters advertise InterCity sleepers, holidays in Britain and the Ideal Home exhibition in London – a long way south.

By the early 1990s the locomotive-hauled trains had gone, replaced by a variety of modern DMU units, such as this Class 156 two-car set, photographed in 1992. They are efficient and practical, but lack character.

LONDON MIDLAND AND SCOTTISH RAILWAY COMPANY.
(HIGHLAND SECTION).
LUGGAGE.
From
TO WICK

This 1950s postcard view of Thurso shows the town and its coastal setting, along with the station in the foreground. The sidings are filled with box vans, a reflection of the importance of freight at that time. Today, Thurso has neither freight nor sidings.

We stayed in the Wick portion of the train and spent a sleepless night in a B&B there, kept awake by almost continuous daylight and screaming gulls who never went to sleep. A bus the next morning took us to Thurso, where we caught the 11.38 and spent almost all day travelling back to Inverness. The return was just as good, as the landscape unrolled in reverse.

If I had to pick Britain's best railway journey, this would probably be it, despite a wealth of other choices. I have visited the line since and although I have never been disappointed, something was lost when the modern DMUs took over the route.

THURSO   D 7899

Wick and Thurso stations date from 1874 and are broadly similar. Both have slated train sheds protecting a single platform, with offices to the side. In this 1959 view, sidings and freight wagons dominate the scene and a lorry has been driven onto the platform to facilitate loading or unloading. Thurso's station building is much the same now, but everything else has gone.

Station scenes

Railway buildings reflect the pride and ambition of the companies that created them. Notable are the imposing office blocks built by major companies, particularly after the formation of the Big Four. I have long admired the powerful LMS HQ in Eversholt Street, beside Euston station, seen here in the 1930s.

Two particular enthusiasms of mine, trains and architecture, meet in the railway station, a building type that seems always to have been central to my life. Early station memories are all to do with trains, but even then I seem to have been aware that Surbiton, where I spent days as a young trainspotter, was something special. Years later, I came to appreciate it as a classic Art Deco building. Otherwise, my early memories are of outings and visits and mostly feature Waterloo, firmly established early in my life as a favourite London terminus. Charing Cross and Victoria figured but, as a complete southerner, I knew nothing about the rest of the big London stations,

I never saw this scene, but wish I had. The photograph of the Coronation Scot at Euston in September 1938 really says it all: a great locomotive on a great express train, surrounded by all the details that bring to life the great days of the railways in Britain. This view of Euston is a reminder that the old station, although a bit of a gloomy muddle, was infinitely better than the 1960s monster we live with now.

L.M.S. OFFICES, LONDON. G.131.

apart from a single visit to Euston prior to its total destruction, to see the prototype Deltic diesel. Naturally, I also remember the Euston arch, as anyone growing up in London in the 1950s was bound to. As a teenager at school in London, architectural interests soon developed, but initially along fairly conventional lines. It took a while for me to appreciate the Victorian period and so, by the time I did, some wonderful buildings had been lost without my noticing them.

Another scene from the glory days, and the morning expresses, including the Flying Scotsman, are lined up waiting to depart from King's Cross. The hats and uniforms suggest it is in the late 1920s.

I found this view of Victoria, taken in July 1927, in an old album. It is simply an excellent station photograph, carefully composed and with wonderful effects of light and shadow. A long line of taxis and two locomotives wait, but the platforms are empty.

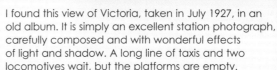
King's Cross

Like most architectural historians, I was brought up to believe that King's Cross was the perfect example of the functional tradition, and a pioneer of modernism. Be that as it may, it is certainly a classic engineer's solution: two grand brick-fronted sheds, representing arrival and departure. I lived near the station for years, so I saw the coming and going of various phases of clutter spoiling the front. This is the 1973 version.

Luckily, I soon came to my senses and began to understand the sheer quality and dynamic originality of Victorian buildings. Of course, stations were high on the list, the Victorians having invented not only a style of exciting diversity but also a completely new building type. From this point, interest in the station began to equal, and then dominate, my enthusiasm for trains. Regardless of personal taste, no one can but be impressed by the astonishing legacy of those famous Victorian architects and, more important, engineers.

By now a habitual train traveller, I increasingly spent much of my life in stations, so I looked at them while waiting for trains. Sometimes, I went simply to look at the station. Work took me all over Britain,

The Great Central, a late arrival on the railway scene, was for that reason a fast main line. Its obliteration in the 1960s stopped it becoming the basis for a new high-speed network. Having explored the route to see what remains, I became aware of the huge losses. Nottingham Victoria was one, leaving only the clock tower as a kind of tombstone. I very much like this photograph of a 1936 excursion, with a GCR classic.

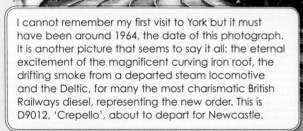

NEVILLE STREET, NEWCASTLE-UPON-TYNE.

Many people collect station postcards and I understand why. I am not a collector, but I do buy cards that excite me. For many architects and engineers, grand stations had to be monuments of classicism, and one of the best is Newcastle Central, by John Dobson, 1850, seen here in the 1930s.

I cannot remember my first visit to York but it must have been around 1964, the date of this photograph. It is another picture that seems to say it all: the eternal excitement of the magnificent curving iron roof, the drifting smoke from a departed steam locomotive and the Deltic, for many the most charismatic British Railways diesel, representing the new order. This is D9012, 'Crepello', about to depart for Newcastle.

The appeal of Penzance is not so much the station, a rather basic structure, but its place at the extreme western end of the British network. I have made the journey many times, and the magic of the long route across Cornwall never lessens. It is a special blend of Brunel echoes with spectacular landscape. The best bit, the view across Mount's Bay, comes right at the end, with Penzance in sight. Here, in October 1973, a Class 52 diesel, D1048, 'Western Lady', is backing out of the platform, having brought in the London train.

Bournemouth is another wonderful station and in this case I could have been there when the photograph was taken, in the 1960s. It is a traditional train shed station and recent restoration (full credit to much abused Railtrack) shows its magnificence. The locomotive, rebuilt Battle of Britain Class No. 34085, is a favourite type.

Living in the West Country now, I spend a lot of time at Bristol Temple Meads, another station that can be enjoyed time and time again. This October 1975 view shows the Torbay Explorer, headed by Class 47 No. 47278, winding through this curving and complex station, in a scene dominated by the vast train shed.

to stations big and small, and I found I enjoyed in equal measure a magnificent structure like Newcastle or a tiny unmanned request halt like Chetnole in Dorset, a classic example of minimal, Southern Railway concrete modernism. I have been lucky to have seen around 80 per cent of Britain's stations, even if many were from a passing train window, along with stations in France and other parts of Europe, North America and Australia. Every station visit now is

Until the 1920s Aberystwyth had a rather inadequate station. The GWR, keen to increase holiday traffic in Wales, built a much grander station. I have often enjoyed the building for its spaciousness and its architectural eccentricity, a kind of vernacular classicism with entertaining details. Today, much of it is used for other things – but at least it is all still there.

Two pictures for Aberystwyth may seem over-generous, but this is more about the decorations than the station. This was for the royal visit in August 1955, and it must have looked splendid as the royal train pulled into the station. Elaborate decorations in this style were normal then. Would anyone bother today?

a treat, even if I have been hundreds of times, and I always look around while waiting, sometimes arriving early to make sure that happens.

Like everyone, I have favourite stations, but that is not really the point. Every station is more than just a building. The architecture is exciting in its diversity, but a station has to work as a complex package of activities and structures in which the trains are just a part. Ultimately it is all about people, and I always enjoy photographs of station life, whatever the era. I also enjoy taking photographs of stations, though nowadays rules and regulations can make this a tricky activity. There is also the particular appeal of derelict,

Fully roofed until 1952, Pickering's 1846 station perfectly explains the term 'train shed' when used to describe a simple through station. As the terminus of the North Yorkshire Moors Railway, it now has a new roof, built to the original designs of GT Andrews, the architectural master of the Northeast. For me, it is the children posing for their father who bring this scene to life.

I used Sevenoaks station often as a schoolboy, but it didn't look like this then. This modern rebuilding dates from the late 1970s, and I like it because it is reflective of British Rail's adventurous approach to station architecture at that time.

abandoned and reused stations, another personal interest, developed while exploring Britain's lost lines. In my books I have used hundreds, possibly even thousands, of station photographs, but there is always room for more. I have chosen the ones shown here for a variety of reasons – architectural interest, history, the quality of the image, personal memories and the infinite curiosity I have about all things to do with railways.

Finally, I have to be honest: it is sometimes about the train that is standing in the station.

For decades a vital, and very common, part of the railway scene, signal boxes are now an endangered species. This, at Worgret Junction, is a good example, serving an area well known to me. It controlled traffic on the Swanage branch, to the west of Wareham.

I do not know Holmgate, but I could not resist this photograph because of its caption: 'Last Passenger from England's Smallest Station'. It looks as though he may have a long wait. What it doesn't say is that Holmgate was a station on the Ashover Light Railway in Derbyshire. Passenger services on the railway ceased completely in 1936, though Holmgate, with its rudimentary shelter, had closed in December 1931.

As someone known to be keen on Victorian Gothic, I am bound to like stations built in variants of the Gothic cottage style. This is Aylesford, an excellent example in Kentish ragstone completed in 1868. The style is vernacular Tudor mixed with fanciful Gothic, and the result is delightful.

Train scenes

Having spent years of my life travelling by train, watching trains and studying thousands of photographs of trains in the course of putting together my books, it would be no surprise to anyone if the result was a grand railway blur. However, some things do stick in the mind, for a variety of reasons, and the images in this chapter illustrate that. The selection was determined by my own memories, historical interest, quirkiness, something particularly evocative or powerful in the image, and pure enjoyment.

If I had to pick the best-looking locomotive of all time, it would have to be GNR No. 1, James Stirling's magnificent 1870 design, with single 8ft 2in driving wheels. The date of this 'official' GNR postcard, about 1912, underlines its lasting reputation.

THE "CORONATION SCOT". L.M.S. Railway.

I am not alone in thinking the 1930s a high point in railway history. It was the era of streamlining, and of battles between the LMS and the LNER. This postcard of the time shows the LMS's Coronation Scot, railway modernism at its best and a triumph of design and engineering.

There is something special about hand-coloured photographs. I have no idea when, where or by whom this classic GWR scene was taken but I could not resist it when I saw it in a pile of old photographs at a railway fair. I am sure there are people who can identify locomotive, location and date, but it doesn't seem to matter to me. It is simply an atmospheric image that captures the great days of steam.

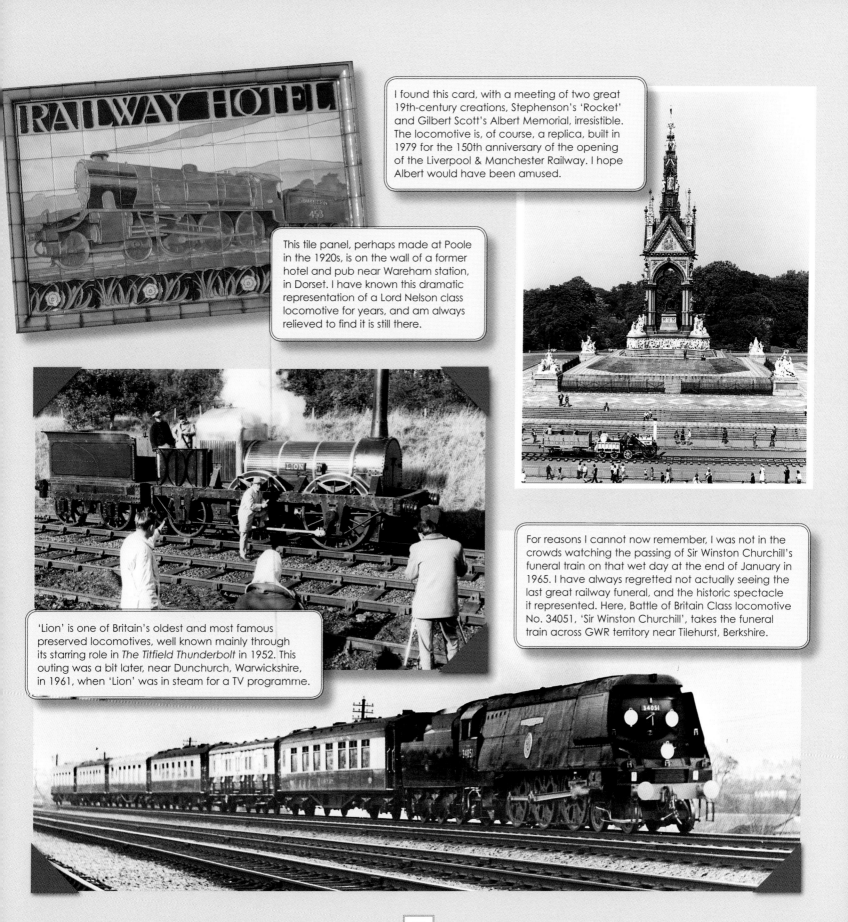

I found this card, with a meeting of two great 19th-century creations, Stephenson's 'Rocket' and Gilbert Scott's Albert Memorial, irresistible. The locomotive is, of course, a replica, built in 1979 for the 150th anniversary of the opening of the Liverpool & Manchester Railway. I hope Albert would have been amused.

This tile panel, perhaps made at Poole in the 1920s, is on the wall of a former hotel and pub near Wareham station, in Dorset. I have known this dramatic representation of a Lord Nelson class locomotive for years, and am always relieved to find it is still there.

For reasons I cannot now remember, I was not in the crowds watching the passing of Sir Winston Churchill's funeral train on that wet day at the end of January in 1965. I have always regretted not actually seeing the last great railway funeral, and the historic spectacle it represented. Here, Battle of Britain Class locomotive No. 34051, 'Sir Winston Churchill', takes the funeral train across GWR territory near Tilehurst, Berkshire.

'Lion' is one of Britain's oldest and most famous preserved locomotives, well known mainly through its starring role in *The Titfield Thunderbolt* in 1952. This outing was a bit later, near Dunchurch, Warwickshire, in 1961, when 'Lion' was in steam for a TV programme.

The naming of locomotives has a long and often fascinating history, and I understand why the nameplates are so keenly collected. My spotting days were in the Southern Region, and I saw plenty of Bulleid Pacifics, developing a fondness for these quirky locomotives that has lasted all my life. This is a magnificent study of the nameplate of rebuilt West Country Class No. 34027, 'Taw Valley'.

Sir Nigel Gresley is one of the most famous names in modern railway history and here it graces one of his class of streamlined A4s, designed by him for the LNER in the 1930s. Always scheduled for preservation, this locomotive is seen here at Derby in September 1974.

This classic study of nameplate, driving wheel and connecting rods, used in a British Railways publicity photograph, is a detail of the Stanier LMS Jubilee Class locomotive No. 45552, 'Silver Jubilee', the first of a large and important class. Sadly, this locomotive was not preserved; it was withdrawn and cut up in 1964.

Diesel nameplates rarely have the same appeal, yet some have historical importance. The first Class 47 diesel locomotive to carry a nameplate was D1666, named in Cardiff in 1965. Later it became 47081, and other number changes followed, but the plates remained on the locomotive until 1990.

Something I find intriguing is the series of locomotive exchange trials in the spring of 1948, when British Railways carried out competitive tests of major locomotives from the pre-nationalization Big Four in order to design their own Standard classes. Here are four 'alien' locomotives working Western Region expresses from Paddington: LMS Class 7P, 'City of Bradford'; LMS Class 6P, 'Queens Westminster Rifleman'; LNER Class A4, 'Mallard'; and SR Merchant Navy Class 'French Line CGT'.

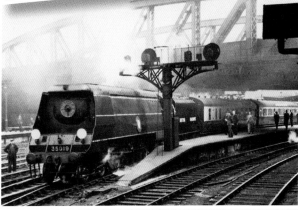

Entitled 'Sunday Morning at Bradford', this is a classic and highly atmospheric steam-age photograph. A study of men attending a locomotive surrounded by steam and smoke on a grimy day, it represents events so commonplace at the time that few bothered to notice, let alone photograph, them. The carriage is filthy, the track is littered with rubbish and the locomotive is destined for the scrapyard.

I have always been amused by the GWR's half-hearted attempts at joining the streamlining revolution in the late 1930s. This view of 'Manorbier Castle' outside the shed at Old Oak Common, West London, shows just how crude the applied streamlining was, achieving little else but spoiling the naturally elegant lines of a Castle Class locomotive.

An old album contained this photograph of 'Mr Drummond's private coupé, taken at Eastleigh 7.9.30'. This famous 4-2-4 inspection saloon was built by the LSWR for Dugald Drummond in 1899 and enjoyed a busy life until it was scrapped in 1940. The coach body survives.

It is all too easy to remember the great locomotives at the expense of the many ordinary, unspectacular engines that kept the network running. This shows one of the Robinson Q4 Class of 0-8-0 goods locomotives, built from 1902, used extensively in the coal trade and seen here hauling empty coal wagons through Nottingham Victoria in about 1930.

Of the many specialist railway vehicles, few were as important, or as exciting, as dynamometer cars. They were used regularly for speed recording throughout the network, but inevitably one thinks of the record-breaking run by LNER No. 4468, 'Mallard', in 1938, and the role played by an LNER car in confirming and recording the speed.

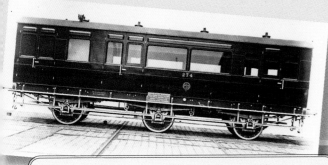

When there were numerous competing railway companies, variety in carriage design was almost infinite. Care was always taken to cater for the needs of all kinds of passengers. This is a six-wheeler Lancashire & Yorkshire invalid saloon, shown at the Royal Jubilee Exhibition of 1887.

This official LNER photograph from the 1930s shows the interior of such an invalid saloon, built in this case by the GNR in about 1900. The comfortable yet casually arranged furniture shows that the needs on a long journey of both invalid and carer were well considered. A number of other specialist vehicles were made for particular family and private needs.

This is the interior of the LNER dynamometer car used in the 1938 'Mallard' world-record run. Complex and precise recording machinery contrasts oddly with padded upholstery and frilly lampshades. One of the technicians had to sit on the piano stool in the foreground – a hint of classic British amateurishness?

A Class 47 diesel hauls a train across the Leeds & Liverpool Canal while a modern steel narrow boat works its way up the locks. The date, the early 1970s, is indicated by the graffiti – 'LFC', 'Vietnam' and 'Slade'. The conjunction between canals and railways is often close, providing an insight into Britain's early industrial history and the need for efficient transport systems.

One of Britain's great stations is Newcastle Central, famous above all for the complexity of tracks leading into the station. This view has been photographed thousands of times, but it is always exciting. Here, a Deltic hauls its train out of the station in the 1980s.

I am not alone in thinking that the line through the centre of Wales, from Caersws to Machynlleth, is one of the best in Britain. In the summer of 1975, passengers rush for the last carriage while the guard waits to get the train away. By the time I first travelled the line, ten years later, short DMUs had replaced locomotive-hauled trains.

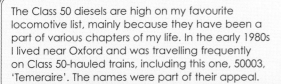

The Class 50 diesels are high on my favourite locomotive list, mainly because they have been a part of various chapters of my life. In the early 1980s I lived near Oxford and was travelling frequently on Class 50-hauled trains, including this one, 50003, 'Temeraire'. The names were part of their appeal.

In 1984 50007, 'Hercules', was repainted in green and renamed 'Sir Edward Elgar' as part of the 150th anniversary celebrations of the GWR. I travelled behind it many times. Later, I moved to Dorset, and the Class 50s came with me, to spend their last years serving West Country routes from Waterloo. When they had gone, I missed their distinctive sound and familiar look.

Another classic image in its own way, this photograph captures Class 40 diesel No. 40091, as its driver carefully reverses it onto a special at Blackpool North in September 1974. The semaphore signals, and the railwayman enjoying his cigarette by the gas cylinders, make an everyday scene memorable.

Another chapter in my life involved regular travel between London and Stoke-on-Trent, on trains hauled by Class 86 electric locomotives. This British Railways publicity photograph shows E3164 when it was brand new, in the late 1960s. Later renumbered 86225, it carried the name 'Hardwicke' between 1980 and 2003, and was then scrapped in 2006.

MYSTERY PHOTOS

THERE ARE MANY legacies of the enthusiasm for railways that has existed since the Victorian era, including societies, books and magazines. However, the greatest by far is the extensive archive of images left by generations of photographers, amateur and professional. Some are household names in the railway world, but many more remain little known or even anonymous. Luckily, most photographs carry on the back a written caption that records the place, time and date. However, many are blank. A few favourites are shown here in the hope that a reader might be able to identify the location.

▼ A mainline railway, busy with freight traffic, curves along the shore of a lake or reservoir in Scotland or the Peak District.

▲ Carefully posed and typically Edwardian, this shows a signal box, a crossing and a grand cottage.

A train of ballast wagons, headed by a Class 7200 heavy freight locomotive, passes through a country station in the Western Region.

A Class 04/8 freight locomotive hauls a train of coal hoppers past a mine in Nottinghamshire or Yorkshire.

▲ This 1930s aerial view shows a massive railway works, possibly St Rollox near Glasgow.

▲ A signal receives attention while a Class 5100 locomotive takes a local stopping service out of a large Western Region station.

▲ A Jubilee, No. 45704, 'Leviathan', stabled at Bolton, makes a smoky departure from a large station in the Midlands or North of England.

▼ *Shafts of sunlight fall on an 8F, two 5MTs and other locomotives in a roundhouse somewhere in May 1952.*

▼ *A snowplough team struggles to clear a rocky cutting during a very hard winter in the 1930s.*

▲ *The same Jubilee, 'Leviathan', here looking rather smarter, makes another smoky departure from another station in northern England.*

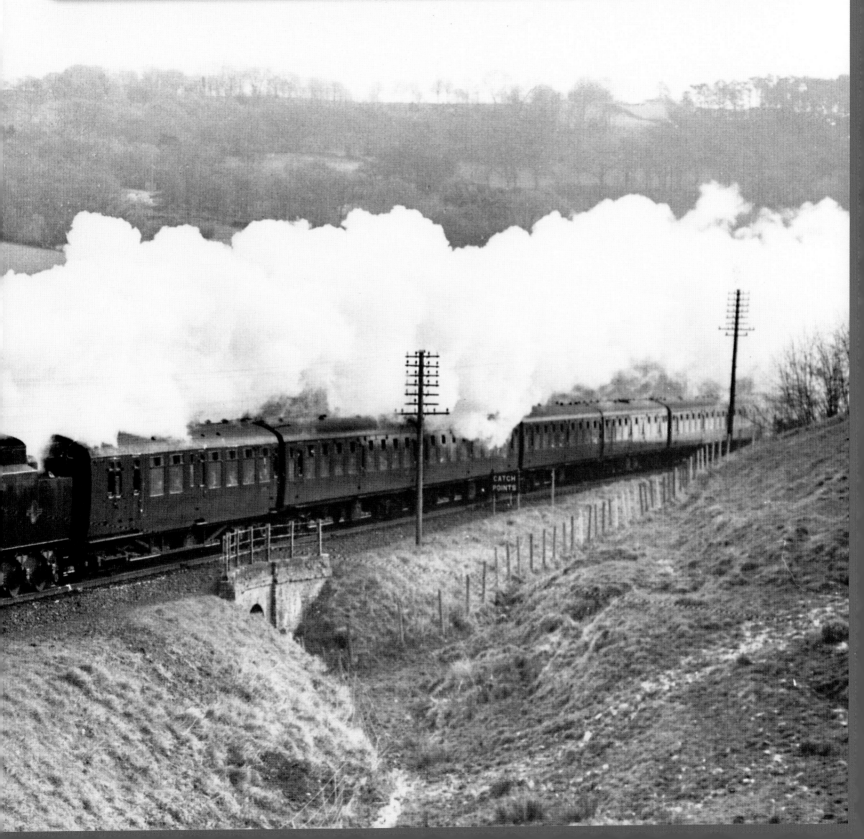

PICTURE FILE

▶ The Royal Albert Bridge is the gateway to Cornwall and, as such, has been regularly photographed since the 1860s. This modern view, taken in 1999, shows a mixed freight, including empty china clay tankers, making its way westwards across the Tamar.

▶ This more traditional view, taken in August 1951, shows another mixed freight going eastwards. The locomotive, an old GWR 4300 Class, No. 6319, has slowed by the signal box for the single-line token to be returned. The view of Brunel's bridge is very much better without the intrusive and dominant road bridge that was opened ten years later.

◄On a wet July day in 1973, with the signalman sheltering in his box, a Penzance-bound express hurries through Par, with Class 52 No. D1054, 'Western Governor', in charge. Within a few years, the locomotive had been scrapped, along with most of the Western class diesels.

▼ In October 1975 the next generation of locomotives has taken over and the Cornish Riviera Limited is ready to depart from Penzance, with Class 50 No. 50039 at its head. In 1978 this locomotive was named 'Implacable'.

▼ In a classic steam-age scene, the 10.51am for Plymouth North Road departs from Launceston on a sunny autumn morning in 1953. The tank locomotive is No. 5567, from the large 4500 Class, whose original design dated back to 1906. Today, nothing remains from this scene.

Southwest England

▶ By 1960 the new diesel multiple units were appearing on lesser routes all over Britain. Here, in September of that year, steam and diesel meet at Saltash on local stopping services. The DMU is departing for Plymouth, while the steam train, headed by GWR Castle Class No. 4087, 'Cardigan Castle', is the Penzance service.

▼ The South Devon hills were a famous challenge for steam locomotive drivers and firemen, and bankers were frequently necessary. In June 1960, a GWR Grange, No. 6875, 'Hindford Grange', tackles Dainton Bank with a mixed freight, including loaded coal wagons. A tank locomotive works hard, banking at the rear.

◀ Elderly locomotives often finished their working lives on shed, station or shunting duties. This Victorian veteran, a Class M7, No. 30667, built originally for the LSWR in about 1897, was spending its last years shunting at Exeter Central when photographed in September 1959.

▼ In August 1956 Tiverton Junction was still a large and busy station, well used to sights like this: a Penzance-bound express races through, headed by a GWR Castle Class locomotive, No. 5038, 'Morlais Castle'. This scene represents British Railways Western Region steam at its best.

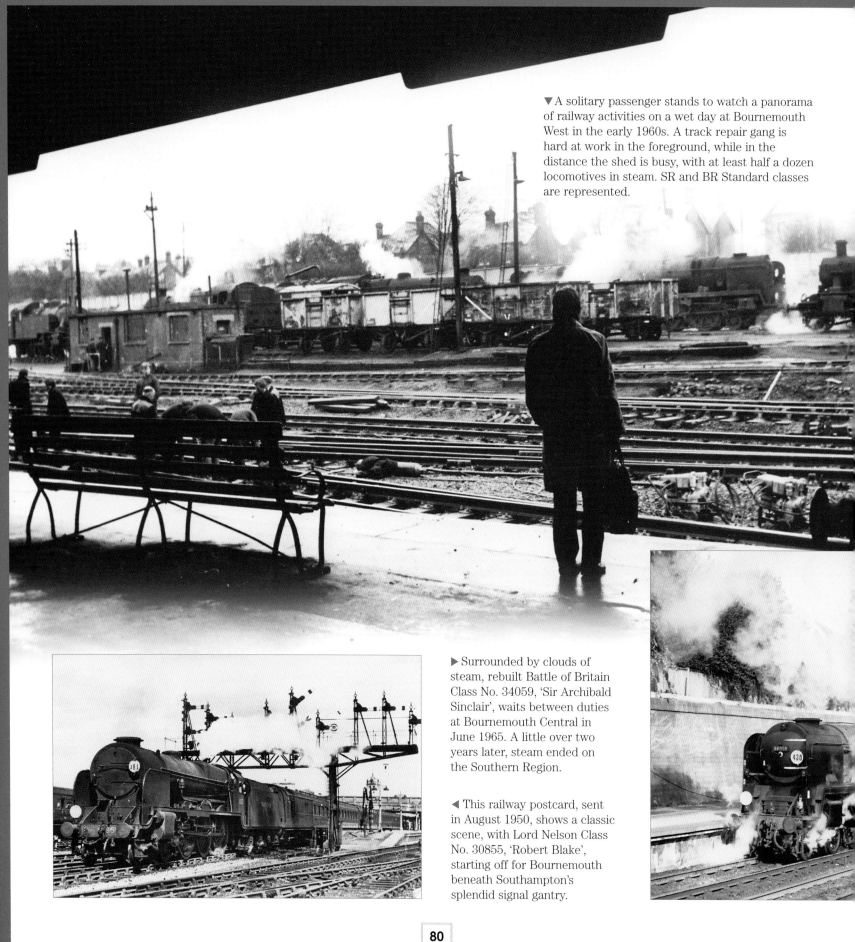

▼ A solitary passenger stands to watch a panorama of railway activities on a wet day at Bournemouth West in the early 1960s. A track repair gang is hard at work in the foreground, while in the distance the shed is busy, with at least half a dozen locomotives in steam. SR and BR Standard classes are represented.

▶ Surrounded by clouds of steam, rebuilt Battle of Britain Class No. 34059, 'Sir Archibald Sinclair', waits between duties at Bournemouth Central in June 1965. A little over two years later, steam ended on the Southern Region.

◀ This railway postcard, sent in August 1950, shows a classic scene, with Lord Nelson Class No. 30855, 'Robert Blake', starting off for Bournemouth beneath Southampton's splendid signal gantry.

Picture file

▶ This deliberately atmospheric photograph is fully captioned: 'Sunday July 7th 1974 – at sunset. Western Advocate speeds through Pilning with the 17.30 Paignton-Cardiff.'

▲ Bristol Parkway is the setting for this 1980s photograph. An HST 125, headed by power car No. 253008, roars away from the station while a ballast train is held by the signals. In the distance the sidings are busy with freight wagons, while in the foreground a solitary railwayman wanders towards the camera, seemingly oblivious of the trains.

LOST LINES

In my trainspotting days, I was most excited by the Southern Region's West Country expresses, and seeing a locomotive bearing the Atlantic Coast Express headboard was a high point. Later, as I came to realize the complexity of the route and the many destinations of this train, it became ever more appealing. It also offered an insight into the competitive world of Victorian railways and the deadly rivalry between

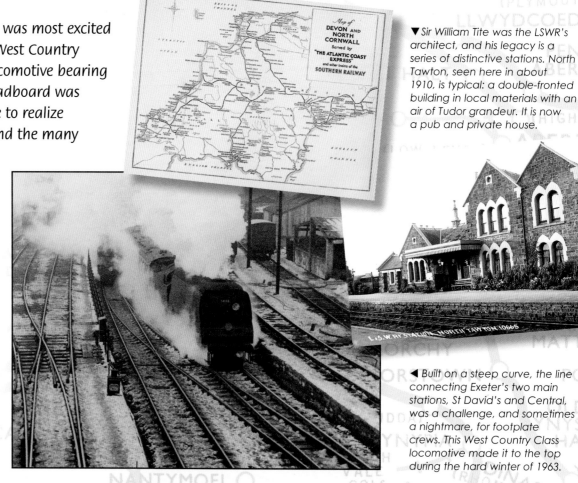

Map of
DEVON AND
NORTH
CORNWALL
Served
by
"THE ATLANTIC COAST
EXPRESS"
and other trains of the
SOUTHERN RAILWAY

▼ Sir William Tite was the LSWR's architect, and his legacy is a series of distinctive stations. North Tawton, seen here in about 1910, is typical: a double-fronted building in local materials with an air of Tudor grandeur. It is now a pub and private house.

No. 32A.

BRITISH RAILWAYS
SOUTHERN REGION

SEPTEMBER 27th, 1948,
and until further notice.

TRAIN SERVICE AND FARES

BETWEEN

WATERLOO

AND

BODMIN
BUDE
CAMELFORD (for Boscastle and Tintagel)
DEVONPORT
HALWILL
HOLSWORTHY
LAUNCESTON
OKEHAMPTON
OTTERHAM
PADSTOW
PLYMOUTH
PORT ISAAC ROAD
TAVISTOCK
WADEBRIDGE

Waterloo Station,
London, S.E.1.

JOHN ELLIOT,
Chief Regional Officer.

Waterlow & Sons Limited,
London & Dunstable.

TW 4372 /—   10,000
1948

◀ Built on a steep curve, the line connecting Exeter's two main stations, St David's and Central, was a challenge, and sometimes a nightmare, for footplate crews. This West Country Class locomotive made it to the top during the hard winter of 1963.

▶ In a classic Atlantic Coast Express scene – and a high point for trainspotters – rebuilt Merchant Navy Class No. 35026, 'Lamport & Holt Line', waits to depart from Exeter Central in the early 1960s.

▼ Okehampton station has seen many changes, from major junction to dereliction and then to restoration. Opened in 1871 and closed to passengers in 1972, the line stayed open for stone trains and the station survived. Now looking better than ever, it is a hub for walkers, cyclists and the occasional train.

▲ This is a view of the approach to Okehampton in the LSWR era. Loco shed, turntable and sidings filled with freight wagons show its importance as a major junction on the route to Devon and Cornwall. Present plans include the possible full restoration of the route to Plymouth, the expansion of freight traffic on the existing line, and the restoration of full passenger services.

▲▶ Dating from the 1870s, Meldon is by far the better of Britain's only two surviving iron trestle viaducts. It is an imposing structure, exciting close to and dramatic within the landscape. It now carries a footpath and cycleway, so is easily enjoyed. Footpaths also pass beneath it.

the GWR and the LSWR, something that defied logic yet survived into the British Railways era. Sadly, much of the route disappeared before I had travelled it. However, I made up for this by getting to know the surviving bits and exploring in depth the lost sections, a process that started in the 1970s and has continued ever since. There have been many changes. Derelict tracks have become footpaths and cycle trails, and abandoned stations have been given new lives. However, nothing has ever altered my affection for the Atlantic Coast Express.

▲ By 1968 the tracks had gone and nature was claiming back much of the route. This is Delabole station, another typical LSWR stone building. It still had both platforms, and someone was camping on the trackbed. Now it survives as a private house, but is surrounded by modern housing.

▲ The route was famous for its landscape and views. On a quiet day at Camelford, perhaps in the 1920s, a couple are enjoying the view towards Launceston while waiting for their train. Camelford station is nowhere near its town, but it was promoted as the stop for Boscastle and Tintagel.

▼ By the mid-1960s the signs of impending closure were all around, but Halwill, the meeting point of four routes, was still busy. On this gloomy day, the diesels were in charge. Nothing survives.

▲ The route of the LSWR's North Cornwall line can be followed, but what remains is highly varied. Some parts are official cycle tracks and walkways, some are informal footpaths, some stretches are inaccessible or impenetrable, and some have vanished altogether. This gorse-filled cutting is near Port Isaac Road.

◀ Between Boscarne Junction and Padstow the route has become one of Britain's most popular cycleways, yet few of the passing cyclists or walkers take the time to explore the old main line towards Launceston. Much has disappeared, but there is still plenty to discover, including this bridge hidden in dense woodland near Wadebridge.

◀ There were many tentacles at the end of the Atlantic Coast Express route, one of which ended at Bude. Here, in September 1923, a smart-looking X6 Class, an Adams LSWR design of 1885, is ready to depart.

▲ In June 1958 this Beattie well tank, No. 30587, was busy shunting at Wadebridge. The last survivors of this ancient class were associated with this area until the 1960s. Built in 1874, this locomotive has been preserved.

▶ The bridge over Petherick Creek survives and is now an exciting feature on the cycleway from Wadebridge to Padstow. This popular route is often busy with cyclists and walkers enjoying the glorious scenery of the Camel as well as the tangible echoes of the railway.

▲ The single-track line from Wadebridge to Padstow followed the Camel estuary, crossing Petherick Creek on a big, curving, girder bridge. It is seen here in about 1910, when it was a major feature of the landscape.

RAILWAY BRIDGE PADSTOW 21528

POSTERS & EPHEMERA

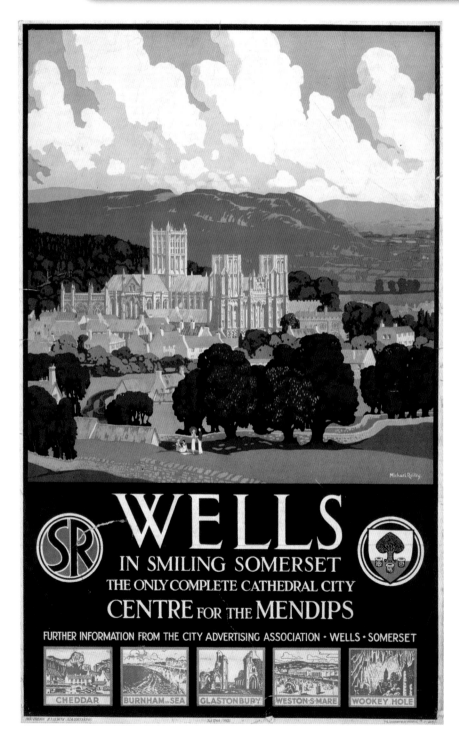

◄ Teignmouth *is* Devon – a BR Western Region poster of 1949 from a painting by Norman Howard

► Weymouth – a BR Southern Region poster of 1960 designed by Laurence Fish

◄ Wells in Smiling Somerset – an SR poster of 1931 from a painting by Michael Reilly

► Bath: The Georgian City – a BR Western Region poster of the early 1960s designed by Chris Watkiss

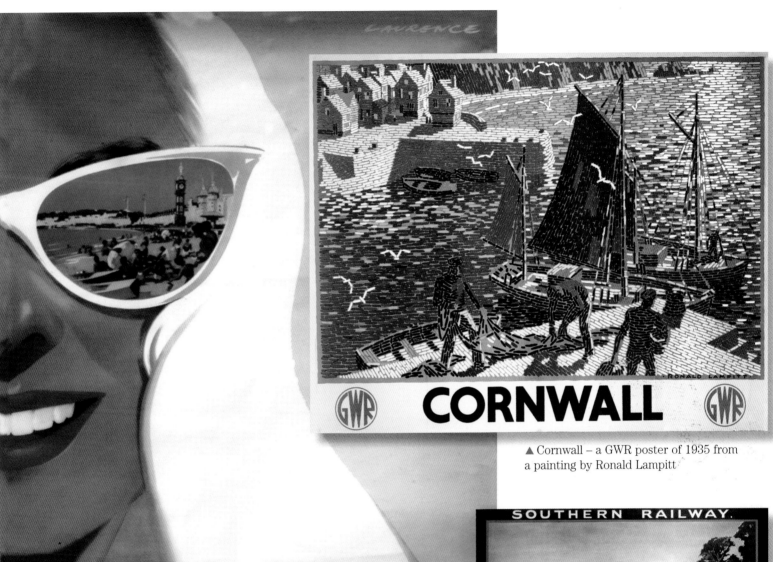

CORNWALL

GWR   GWR

Weymouth

DORSET

GO BY TRAIN

OFFICIAL GUIDE (1/-) FROM PUBLICITY DEPT., 101 ALEXANDRA GARDENS, WEYMOUTH, DORSET.

▲ Cornwall – a GWR poster of 1935 from a painting by Ronald Lampitt

SOUTHERN RAILWAY.

THIS BIT OF COAST COMMENCES JUST EAST OF LYME REGIS (DORSET) AND EXTENDS PAST THE LANDSLIP (DEVON), SEATON, SIDMOUTH, BUDLEIGH SALTERTON TO EXMOUTH, WITH DARTMOOR IN THE BACKGROUND. IT IS TYPICAL OF THE MANY CHARMING HOLIDAY REGIONS TO WHICH THE SOUTHERN RAILWAY PROVIDES ACCESS BY EXPRESS RESTAURANT CAR TRAINS.

▲ Southern Railway – an SR poster of the early 1920s promoting the Dorset and Devon coast route (artist unknown)

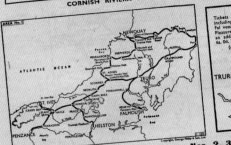

◄▲► In the 19th century the Southwest was the setting for many battles between the GWR and the LSWR, establishing a rivalry that was maintained into the British Railways era. Although freight was important, the competition was really for the expanding holiday traffic. The Great Western named South Devon and Cornwall 'The English Riviera', and the Southern replied with its ACE, or Atlantic Coast Express. Publicity was adventurous and attractive, with plenty of excursions, tours and special tickets, and brochures promoting the complete holiday package.

"*Through the Window*
PADDINGTON to PENZANCE
GREAT·WESTERN RAILWAY
PRICE·ONE SHILLING

G. W. R.
FOWEY

London and South Western Ry.
TO
POOLE

SOUTHERN
WHIT SUNDAY JUNE 5th
REFRESHMENT CAR EXCURSION
To
Salisbury, Yeovil, Lyme Regis,
Seaton, Exeter, Sidmouth,
Exmouth, etc.

▲▶ 'Through the Window' guides were always popular, highlighting both landscape features and places of interest, and helping the long journeys to pass. Many of the resorts in the Southwest were dependent on the railways for their business, so joint marketing ventures were common. Until the 1970s, excursions were always popular, and the railways used them as a way to attract traffic to some lesser-used routes, such as the old Somerset & Dorset line.

(S)
6M.   (787)
BRITISH RAILWAYS
FROM WATERLOO TO
MORTEHOE

TRAVEL TO

Plymouth
The Holiday centre for Devon & Cornwall

THE SUN

PLEASE RETAIN THIS PAMPHLET FOR FURTHER REFERENCE

Attractive Regular
EXCURSIONS

from

BATH (Green Park), RADSTOCK NORTH
MIDSOMER NORTON SOUTH
CHILCOMPTON
SHEPTON MALLET (Charlton Road)
EVERCREECH Jct, COLE, WINCANTON
and INTERMEDIATE STATIONS

18th JUNE, 1962 to 9th SEPTEMBER, 1962
(INCLUSIVE)   (OR UNTIL FURTHER NOTICE)

The Train Services in this pamphlet are subject to alteration or cancellation at short notice and do not necessarily apply at Bank or Public Holidays. Passengers should confirm beforehand the service on which they intend to travel.

BRITISH RAILWAYS

RAILWAY POSTCARDS

① SR's Atlantic Coast Express depicted in the 1920s

② GWR 'official card' of Lynmouth c.1910

③ Edwardian view of the LSWR's Plymouth express

④ GWR 'official card' of Weymouth posted in 1910

⑤ Edwardian view of Bude, an LSWR Cornish outpost

⑥ Classic card of the Royal Albert Bridge, Saltash, posted in 1915

⑦ 1905 card showing the incline on the Portreath branch

⑧ Edwardian view of Bournemouth's 1880s Central station

⑨ GWR 'official card' of Penzance posted in 1908

THE ESPLANADE, WEYMOUTH.
GREAT WESTERN RAILWAY.

S 11701   APPROACH TO L. & S. W. RLY STATION, BUDE.

Saltash Bridge

Portreath showing Cable Railway.

The Central Railway Station.

BOURNEMOUTH

THE PARADE, PENZANCE.

SHEDS & WORKS

THE NETWORK of more than 300 major locomotive sheds, built to cater for day-to-day operation and maintenance, was a crucial component of the steam age. The major ones, to which numbers of locomotives were allocated, were identified by a number and letter code, usually in the form of an iron plate carried on the locomotive smokebox door. When steam ended, most sheds immediately became redundant. Though some could handle heavy repairs and overhauls, this was usually the province of specialist works.

▲ *(Top) The classic type of shed is the roundhouse, with locomotives stabled on tracks radiating from a central turntable. Aberdare shed in South Wales (86J, later 88J) was a roundhouse-type shed, though not in the traditional circular building. At its peak it looked after over 40 locomotives, mostly for the local coal traffic, with some typical GWR classes represented in this 1960s photograph.*

▲ *Another roundhouse was York (50A), inevitably the home of some famous mainline locomotives. Stabled side by side here in the 1960s were two great designs from the LNER era: (left) a 1940s Class A2, No. 60532, 'Blue Peter', and (right) a Class A4, No. 60019, 'Bittern'. Both of these were scheduled for preservation.*

▲ In 1922 the GWR acquired fifteen locomotives formerly owned by the Burry Port & Gwendraeth Valley Railway, a tiny South Wales company dating from the 1860s. Two were 0-6-0 tanks built by Hudswell Clarke in 1909, one of which, No. 2197, can be seen here in Llanelli shed (87F) during the British Railways era. It carried the name 'Pioneer'.

▲ The former GWR Old Oak Common shed (81A) was another roundhouse, serving London's Paddington station. Here, a 1960s line-up of the residents includes Hall Class No. 6937, 'Conyngham Hall', and 4700 Class No. 4703.

▼ This excellent study of a GWR classic shows a well-cared-for Castle Class locomotive, No. 7023, 'Penrice Castle', getting ready for a day's work outside Worcester shed (85A) in August 1962. The coal is piled high and the locomotive is waiting its turn at the water tower. Beyond, the lines of coal wagons, the crane and the rather scruffy GWR pannier tank hint at the complexity of maintaining a busy locomotive shed.

In 1955 one of a small class of dock shunters, built by the GWR in 1910 to a Churchward design, takes water outside Laira shed near Plymouth (83D). All five members of the class passed into British Railways ownership and, judging by the condition of this one, No. 1361, they were well cared for. They usually worked around Millbay Docks and the Sutton Harbour branch. One member of the class, No. 1363, has been preserved.

▲ The largest sheds were equipped with automated coaling towers, such as this example, seen at Stoke-on-Trent in 1936 shortly after completion.

◄ By 1983 few sheds were still standing, let alone in use, because diesel locomotives were regularly stabled in the open. This is Stoke-on-Trent again, with four Class 25 diesels standing in the December sunshine in Cockshute sidings. In the background is Twyford's sanitary works.

◀ Swindon, established by the GWR in 1841 and closed in 1986, was one of Britain's largest and longest-lasting railway works. This 1950s photograph shows part of Swindon's 11-acre A shop, the centre of locomotive building. A number of famous locomotives, including 'Goodrich Castle', are undergoing a major overhaul.

▼ Laira, near Plymouth, equipped as it was for heavy engineering, was more than just a locomotive shed. Built originally in the late 1840s, it became a major locomotive shed and maintenance centre from 1901. It was rebuilt to look after diesels from the early 1960s and became famous as the home of the Class 52 Western diesels, two of which, 'Western Hussar' and 'Western Trooper', are seen here under repair in June 1970.

INDUSTRY

THE EARLIEST railways were industrial lines, usually associated with mining and quarrying. From these roots grew a vast network of dedicated industrial railways, serving not only coal mines, stone, slate, clay and other quarries, but also brickworks, gasworks, breweries, harbours, docks and much else. The earliest locomotives were built for industry, and various manufacturers, including Manning Wardle and Hunslet, specialized in the generally small locomotives required. Steam survived on industrial lines well into the 1970s.

◄ Until it was destroyed in the 1980s, coal mining was the major user of industrial railways, and scenes like this were commonplace throughout the coalfields. This is Ashington, in the northeast of England, in April 1968, and a 1956 Hunslet saddle tank is hard at work hauling a train of old wooden coal wagons onto the main line near the No.1 loop signal box.

▼ Another Ashington view, this time on a snowy February day in 1970, shows a 1954 Hunslet making a smoky departure from the coal sidings with a train of mixed coal wagons. By this time, steam had vanished from the mainline network.

▲ Many National Coal Board locomotives were well maintained and presented, reflecting the sense of pride traditionally associated with the coal-mining industry. This Andrew Barclay locomotive belonging to the West Ayr region was probably built in the 1920s, but was still looking immaculate when this photograph was taken about 40 years later. The ancient plank wagon is a bit of a let-down, but it would have been kept only for internal use around the pit.

▲ This large, heavy duty, 0-6-0 tank was built by Hawthorn Leslie in 1921 and is seen here 50 years later, in October 1971, still in service as No. 9 in the Hartley Main Collieries fleet. This large company operated a number of pits in the northeast of England, in the Cramlington and Seaton Delaval area.

▼ In another West Ayr region scene from the late 1960s or early 1970s, two Andrew Barclay saddle tanks are at work in the sidings on the Waterside coal-mining complex, adjacent to the Ayr & Dalmellington Railway.

▲ Many local gasworks had industrial railway lines and their own locomotives, used for the movement of coal and coke. This well-cared-for Andrew Barclay of 1920 enjoyed a long life as No. 5 in the Bow gasworks fleet, in east London.

◄ The stone industry relied heavily on railways, and many companies had their own locomotives. This 1953 photograph shows 'Elizabeth', an Andrew Barclay 0-4-0 of 1917, in use in Leicestershire with the Croft Granite, Brick & Concrete Company, famous among other things for reconstituted stone mouldings. The driver smiles for the photographer.

▲ Locomotives working on industrial lines often enjoyed long lives, either because their work and their mileage was quite limited or because they were retired into industry after mainline use. As a result, photographs like this are quite common – but always intriguing. The history of this mid-Victorian veteran is not known, and no maker's plate is visible. The driver and the veteran shunter suggest the photograph dates from the 1880s.

▼ Industrial locomotives came in many shapes and sizes, and a number were specially built for particular purposes or locations. This is No. 20 from the fleet at Beckton Gas Works, east London. Built by Neilson and Company of Glasgow, it had a low profile to enable it to pass beneath the gas retorts. The works, opened in 1870, had an extensive railway system connected to the Great Eastern main line at North Woolwich.

▲ One of the batch of famous Terrier tank engines built by the LB&SCR in the 1870s was sold by the Southern Railway to the Newhaven Harbour Company. This was 'Fenchurch', which later returned to the SR, was taken over by British Railways and was subsequently preserved.

▲ This ancient Class 0F saddle tank started life on the Midland Railway in 1883. It lived on through the LMS era and then became British Railways 41615. Seen here in the 1950s, it worked as an industrial shunter.

▲ Another survivor from an earlier age is this vertical-boilered industrial locomotive, probably built for quarry use. The maker and the location are unrecorded, but the number, 201, suggests a large fleet in a major enterprise. De Winton and Sentinel both built vertical-boilered locomotives, the former generally for use in Welsh quarries.

▼ When they came to the end of their lives, industrial locomotives were often abandoned on remote sidings, or partially scrapped and cannibalized for spare parts. This photograph, taken at the Penryn Slate Quarry in North Wales in 1962, shows the rusting remains of 'Stanhope', a narrow gauge quarry locomotive built by Kerr Stuart in 1917.

▲ This is another 1970s scene at Ashington in Northeast England, but it features a diesel locomotive. Originally it was one of 56 Class 14 Paxman-engined shunters built by British Railways at Swindon in the early 1960s. After a very short time in BR service, a number were sold to the National Coal Board, including this example, formerly D9312, seen here still carrying its BR crest.

SOUTHERN ENGLAND

PICTURE FILE

◀ The Didcot, Newbury & Southampton Railway was authorized in 1873 to build a line linking Didcot with Southampton. Progress was slow because of tortuous negotiations with the GWR and the LSWR, over whose tracks much of the route was to run. Winchester was reached in 1885, but the link with the LSWR near Shawford, just south of the city, was not completed until October 1891. When this card, which shows the junction, was posted in Alresford in 1907, the line was still quite new and the 32-arched, brick viaduct clearly visible.

▼ By August 1960, when this photograph was taken, the GWR route through Winchester Chesil station was little more than a country railway. Here, with several passengers leaning out to enjoy the view, a rather tired 1930s Class 2251 locomotive, No. 2240, hauls its three carriages across the junction with the former LSWR line and onto the main line, to complete its leisurely journey to Southampton. The viaduct, known as Hockley, or Shawford, still stands. Since the line's closure in 1966, it has become much more hidden by vegetation but can be seen at close quarters from a nearby footpath.

▲ Introduced by the Southern Railway in 1931, the Bournemouth Belle was an all-Pullman service that ran initially at weekends and then daily. It was withdrawn in July 1967. In May 1959 Merchant Navy Class No. 35027, 'Port Line', takes the Belle through Vauxhall, London, at the start of the journey.

▲ In the mid-1960s steam was coming to an end on the Southern Region and the surviving locomotives often looked tired and uncared for. This is rebuilt West Country Class No. 34047, 'Callington', taking water on a wet day at Southampton. The driver is keeping an eye on the proceedings.

▲ Network SouthEast's livery always looked a bit odd on trains running to the West Country. This is Class 50 No. 50003, 'Temeraire', on an Exeter service near Clapham Junction in 1990.

◀ This photograph was taken in June 1967, by which point steam was a rarity at Clapham Junction. However, there were still some unusual things to be seen. Here, just one month before the end of steam on Southern Railway, an LMS-designed Class 2MT tank locomotive, No. 41312, heads a rake of Southern Region carriages. The few people on the platform do not seem to be interested, but this train to Kensington Olympia was in fact the last steam-hauled local service in London.

◀ While his mother notes down the number, a small boy is tense with excitement at the sight of an ancient Class K locomotive, No. 32342, built originally for the London, Brighton & South Coast Railway. It is August 1956, and the locomotive is waiting to leave Newick & Chailey en route to Brighton via Lewes. The Bluebell Railway now operates over a section of this route.

▼ One of the quirkiest locomotive designs was Bulleid's Austerity Class Q1, introduced by the Southern Railway in 1942 for heavy wartime freight working. There were 40 in the class, the last being withdrawn in 1966. This 1962 photograph shows No. 33030 passing through Tilehurst with a mixed freight for the Southern Region.

Picture file

▶ The LSWR developed a major new freight facility at Feltham from about 1911, in order to simplify and rationalize the exchange of freight wagons between companies serving different parts of Britain. This was to become one of the best-equipped yards in Britain. In 1954, it was still at work when this Class H16 locomotive, No. 30520, hauled a mixed freight out of the Feltham yard, passing a new Class 08 shunter.

◀ Many freight workhorses had long lives. This 0-6-0, heading a long line of box vans, was probably over 50 years old when the photograph was taken. It is C Class No. 31589, a Wainwright design first introduced by the South Eastern Railway in 1900.

▼ On 21 December 1962 the daily freight from Midhurst to Horsham paused at Petworth. The train comprised a container, three mineral wagons, a plank truck and the brake van, hauled by another long-lived veteran, Class E4 No. 32469, whose design dated back to the Victorian era. Regular local freights such as this were the backbone of the national network.

◄ Early in 1961 a photographer at London King's Cross captured this meeting of two great locomotives that represented past and future. In the distance is a famous classic, an LNER A4, No. 60028, 'Walter K. Whigham', overshadowed by the gleaming Deltic D9003, 'Meld', brand new and smartly painted in its two-tone green livery.

▲ This British Railways publicity photograph from the late 1950s shows the Mid-Day Scot waiting to depart from Euston. The locomotive is Princess Coronation Class No. 46251, 'City of Nottingham'. At this time the train ran non-stop to Carlisle.

▲ King's Cross again, and this time it is another famous LNER design, Class A1 No. 60148, 'Aboyeur', waiting to depart for the North in the early 1960s.

▶ By 1954 London Blackfriars was a minor station handling suburban and domestic services, far from its glory days in the Edwardian era, when it was the starting point of boat trains for European destinations. This unusual steam visitor is a preserved locomotive heading a special for the Inter Regional Ramblers.

Picture file

▲ The locomotive exchanges of 1948 must have been a trainspotter's dream, with many sightings of locomotives in unfamiliar settings. Here, the driver watches nervously as Class A4 No. 60033, 'Seagull', starts a Southern Region express out of Waterloo.

▶ The Class 33 diesels, popularly known as Cromptons, were seen all over the South of England from the 1960s to the 1990s. Here, in 1985, No. 33012 takes a mixed freight past Eastleigh. This locomotive has since been preserved, along with 25 other class members.

▲ In 1958, a year after returning to regular service, a gleaming 'City of Truro' rests at Paddington, having arrived with a Ffestiniog Railway special. The 1903 GWR locomotive, which has been preserved since 1931, was famed as the first to exceed 100mph, though this has since been questioned.

▼ In 1977 the Class 253 HST 125s were still a relative novelty on Western Region services in and out of Paddington, and it is easy now to forget the impact these high-speed diesel multiple unit trains made when first introduced. Here, the 08.48 from Weston-super-Mare passes Westbourne Park on its way into Paddington, while a Class 31 takes empty stock away from the station.

LOST LINES

rowing up on the Kent and Surrey border, and being a keen trainspotter, I should have been familiar with my local lines. However, even in the early 1950s, we seemed to go everywhere in various old cars, so spotting opportunities were rare. By the time railways were being threatened with closure in the 1960s, I was living elsewhere. As a result, I never travelled on many of the lines in this area. Thanks to my fascination with lost railways, I have now explored some of them, including the rural route from Guildford to Brighton via Christ's Hospital, near Horsham, and Shoreham-by-Sea.

One of several ways to get to Brighton from London, this line grew out of rivalry between Victorian railway

▲ Guildford, the county town of Surrey, has always been a busy place, and a popular shopping centre, as this 1920s card suggests. The Guildhall, with its projecting clock, still dominates the High Street. Prior to the railway, the town relied extensively on the Wey Navigation for its trade.

▲ Guildford station, seen here in the 1950s, was opened in 1845 but substantially enlarged in the 1880s. The meeting point for several routes, it remained unchanged until a complete rebuilding in the 1980s.

▶ Much of Bramley & Wonersh station survives, including nameboard, signal, platform, and crossing gates. A plaque commemorates 16 December 1942, when eight passengers were killed in a German air attack on a train in the station.

▲ Baynards station was renamed Valleywood for this filming session, perhaps in the early 1960s. The 1865 station, famous for its floral displays, lived on after the line was closed and is now a private house. A siding served the local brickworks.

Slinfold Station, L. B. & S. C. Ry. Sussex.

◀ Rudgwick was a remote station serving a small village, yet this early 20th-century photograph shows how dependent on the railway such places were. The sidings are full with wagons catering for local traffic, and a goods train is approaching the platform. Nothing remains today.

▲ In this Edwardian view of Slinfold, a few passengers and a porter with parcels await the train. It was always a secondary route, and much of it was built by the LB&SCR as single track. Despite this, a poster advertises trips to Paris. The station site is now a caravan park.

◀ This elegant bridge, built from local brick and complete with the insulators that carried the telegraph wires, survives near Cranleigh, one of the larger towns on the northern part of the route. The old trackbed, now a well-defined path surrounded by greenery, is typical of the Downs Link, which follows the course of the disused railway for most of its route.

companies. It was built in the 1860s by the LB&SCR, keen to encroach on LSWR territory, in two sections – Guildford to Christ's Hospital, and Christ's Hospital to Shoreham. The northern section closed in June 1965, and the busier, southern section nine months later. After a period of abandonment, much of the line was brought back to life in 1984 as the Downs Link, a cycleway, bridleway and footpath connecting the North and South Downs Ways. It is easy to explore this pleasant green corridor, and stations, bridges and echoes of the local brick industry, important in the route's history, can be seen.

▲ South of Christ's Hospital, the track is wider, reflecting the greater importance of the line. West Grinstead was a minor station, with wooden buildings and facilities for handling horse traffic. Today the platforms have been retained, along with other relics, including a carriage.

▶ Popular in Victorian times was Mr Potter's Museum of Curiosities, a building in local flint and brick housing tableaux of stuffed birds and animals dressed as humans. To cater for the number of visitors, an extension was built onto the platform at Bramber station.

▼ By the summer of 1965 the northern section had closed and the southern part had only a few months to go. Steyning station is packed with enthusiasts on a Locomotive Club of Great Britain railtour, headed by an unusual visitor to the line, Battle of Britain Class No. 34050, 'Royal Observer Corps'.

▲ Many things survive along the route, for example this Southern Railway gradient post, because the transition from railway to official footpath happened quite quickly. Other things, such as signals, have sometimes been brought back in order to enhance the railway atmosphere.

▶ Railway paths are always more enjoyable when original features like this bridge remain in use. When lines were closed, there was often a policy to remove iron bridges, partly for scrap and partly to make it harder to reopen the route. Some survived because the cost of removal was greater than the scrap value.

▶ At Shoreham the line joined the main line along the coast to Brighton, the destination for most trains from Guildford and Christ's Hospital. The grandeur of Brighton station is apparent in this Edwardian card.

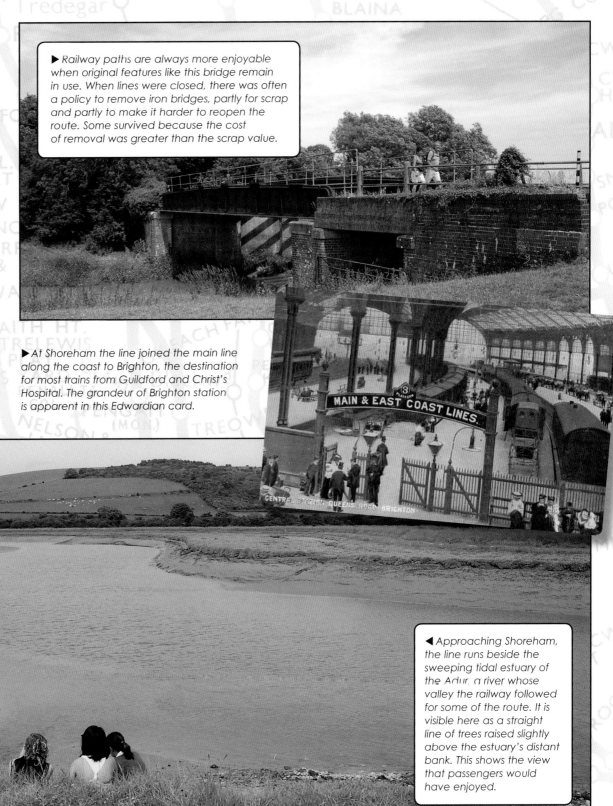

◀ Approaching Shoreham, the line runs beside the sweeping tidal estuary of the Adur, a river whose valley the railway followed for some of the route. It is visible here as a straight line of trees raised slightly above the estuary's distant bank. This shows the view that passengers would have enjoyed.

POSTERS & EPHEMERA

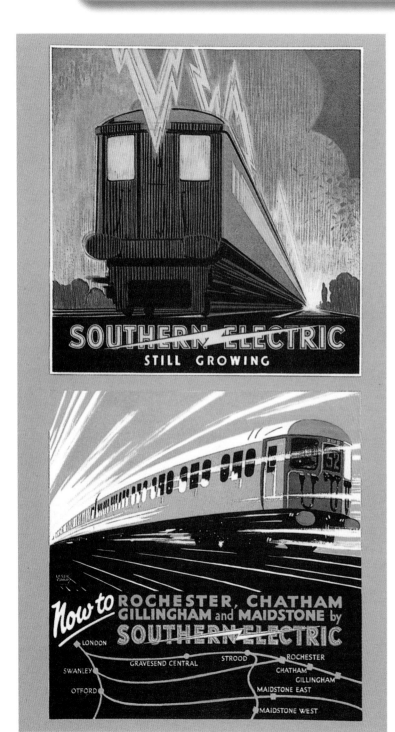

◄ Southern Electric: Still Growing – an SR poster of the 1930s (artist unknown)

▲ London for State Occasions – a Southern Electric poster of the 1930s from a painting by Christopher Clark

RACING OFF RYDE

The narrow water between the mainland and the Isle of Wight is crossed by a regular service of BRITISH RAILWAYS ships from Portsmouth and Lymington

◀ Racing off Ryde –
a BR Southern Region
poster of the late
1950s from a painting
by Claude Buckle

▶ Brighton: For Health
& Pleasure All the Year
Round – an LB&SCR
poster of 1920 from a
painting by Elijah Cox

BRIGHTON
FOR HEALTH & PLEASURE ALL THE YEAR ROUND
For Illustrated Guide (Postage 2½d.) Apply Public Library Brighton: Particulars of Train
Service, Etc. on application to Publicity Dept. L.B.& S.C.Rly. London Bridge Terminus. S.E.1

▶ Live in Surrey and Be
Happy! – an SR poster of 1932
from a painting by Basil White

LIVE IN SURREY
AND BE HAPPY!
FREQUENT ELECTRIC TRAINS DAY AND NIGHT.
"THE COUNTRY AT LONDON'S DOOR,"
FREE AT ANY S.R. ENQUIRY OFFICE.

SOUTHERN

H. A. WALKER,   GENERAL MANAGER.

PORTSMOUTH AND SOUTHSEA

GO BY TRAIN

HOLIDAY GUIDE (3d. P.O.) FROM ENQUIRY OFFICE, CASTLE BUILDINGS, SOUTHSEA, HANTS.

▲ Portsmouth and Southsea: Go by Train – a BR
Southern Region poster of 1960 from a design
by Laurence Fish

(37)
North British Railway.

King's Cross
(LONDON)

BRITISH RAILWAYS
EASTERN REGION
(O.S. 7348)

PASSENGERS FOR

FENCHURCH STREET ONLY

CONVEYED IN THIS CARRIAGE

London Brighton & South Coast Railway.
167 (54a)

TO

Shoreham-by-Sea

HINTS
FOR
HOLIDAYS

ISLE
OF
WIGHT
Section

SOUTHERN
RAILWAY

◄ ▼ ► Holidays and excursions to and from London were big business for the Southern Railway and its many predecessors, some of whose names feature on the luggage labels here. Typical were the many special trains for the annual Aldershot Tattoo. British Railways carried on with excursion traffic but, as this diminished, the emphasis switched to off-peak travel and the promotion of famous brands such as InterCity.

JULY
AUGUST
SEPTEMBER

EXCURSIONS
FROM
KING'S CROSS
LIVERPOOL STREET
AND
FENCHURCH STREET
14th JUNE to 31st JULY
INCLUSIVE

for cheap facilities to race meetings and other sporting events
see separate announcements

BRITISH RAILWAYS

A 167

INTERCITY
SAVERS
FROM
LONDON

From 4 October 1987
until further notice.

For Days out – or stay away
up to a month.

Discovering London
by Inter-City

Kent & East Sussex Railway

PERISHABLE

SOUTHERN RAILWAY
(7/47) 12M
TO
Stock
787
CHICHESTER

HORSMONDEN

SOUTHERN RAILWAY
(12/46) 12M
TO
Stock
787
DEAL

London and South Western Ry.
787
FROM WATERLOO TO
NORBITON

Inter-City makes the going easy

IN AID OF MILITARY CHARITABLE FUNDS

THE TATTOO · ALDERSHOT

7·8·9·10 and 13·14·15·16·17·JUNE 1939

"Take my drum to England, hang et by the Shore,
Strike et when your powder's runnin' low;"—"*Drake's Drum*," Newbolt.

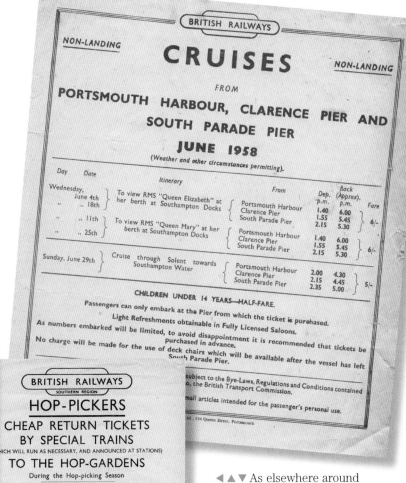

BRITISH RAILWAYS

NON-LANDING

CRUISES

NON-LANDING

FROM
PORTSMOUTH HARBOUR, CLARENCE PIER AND
SOUTH PARADE PIER
JUNE 1958
(Weather and other circumstances permitting).

Day	Date	Itinerary	From	Dep. p.m.	Back (Approx.) p.m.	Fare
Wednesday,	June 4th	To view RMS "Queen Elizabeth" at	Portsmouth Harbour	1.40	6.00	
,,	,, 18th	her berth at Southampton Docks	Clarence Pier	1.55	5.45	
			South Parade Pier	2.15	5.30	6/-
,,	,, 11th	To view RMS "Queen Mary" at her	Portsmouth Harbour	1.40	6.00	
,,	,, 25th	berth at Southampton Docks	Clarence Pier	1.55	5.45	
			South Parade Pier	2.15	5.30	6/-
Sunday, June 29th		Cruise through Solent towards Southampton Water	Portsmouth Harbour	2.00	4.30	
			Clarence Pier	2.15	4.45	
			South Parade Pier	2.35	5.00	5/-

CHILDREN UNDER 14 YEARS—HALF-FARE.

Passengers can only embark at the Pier from which the ticket is purchased.

Light Refreshments obtainable in Fully Licensed Saloons.

As numbers embarked will be limited, to avoid disappointment it is recommended that tickets be purchased in advance.

No charge will be made for the use of deck chairs which will be available after the vessel has left South Parade Pier.

... subject to the Bye-Laws, Regulations and Conditions contained ... the British Transport Commission.

... mall articles intended for the passenger's personal use.

... 154 Queen Street, Portsmouth

BRITISH RAILWAYS
SOUTHERN REGION
HOP-PICKERS
CHEAP RETURN TICKETS
BY SPECIAL TRAINS
(WHICH WILL RUN AS NECESSARY, AND ANNOUNCED AT STATIONS)
TO THE HOP-GARDENS
During the Hop-picking Season
PASSENGERS WILL RECEIVE ADVICE CARDS FROM THE FARMERS AND SHOULD ACT STRICTLY IN ACCORDANCE WITH THE INSTRUCTIONS GIVEN THEREON.

To FAVERSHAM and SELLING

FROM	RETURN FARES, THIRD CLASS, TO:—	
	FAVERSHAM	SELLING
	s. d.	s. d.
LONDON BRIDGE	9/11	10/7
WOOLWICH ARSENAL	8/6	9/2
DARTFORD	7/7	7/7
GRAVESEND CENTRAL	5/5	6/1
CHATHAM	3/7	4/5
GILLINGHAM (KENT)	3/4	4/2

To WROTHAM, MALLING and MAIDSTONE

FROM	RETURN FARES, THIRD CLASS, TO :—			
	WROTHAM & BOROUGH GREEN	WEST MALLING	EAST MALLING HALT	MAIDSTONE EAST
	s. d.	s. d.	s. d.	s. d.
HOLBORN VIADUCT	6/2	7/4	7/6	8/3
BLACKFRIARS	6/1	7/3	7/4	8/3
ELEPHANT & CASTLE	5/11	7/-	7/3	8/-
LOUGHBOROUGH JUNCTION	5/7	6/6	6/10	7/7
PENGE EAST	4/8	5/8	5/11	6/10

CHILDREN 3 AND UNDER 14 YEARS, HALF-FARE.

TICKETS AVAILABLE ONLY FOR RETURN BY SPECIAL TRAINS AS ANNOUNCED AT STATIONS IN HOP-PICKING AREAS.

Hop-pickers' luggage, etc., cannot be accepted for deposit in the Cloak Rooms at the under-mentioned stations.

... London Bridge ... Woolwich Arsenal
... New Cross ... Gravesend Central
... New Cross Gate ... Chatham

... Luggage on the Platform, and see it is marked with the ...
... Labels, showing plainly Owner's Name and Address, also ...
... cepted for conveyance by Railway.
... loss, damage or delay to such Luggage.
... accepted as Passengers' Luggage.

... ued as less than the ordinary fares and are ...
... e publications of the Railway Executive, or the ...

Printed in Great Britain by:
J. W. Owen, Maldon Road, Chess, Surrey.

◀▼ Unusually, an Official LNWR Card showing Harrow signal box was overprinted by a Mr Pembrook to advertise his coal, coke and corn business in Deal, rather than something more local.

▼ As elsewhere around the network, cheaply produced handbills distributed at stations and booking offices were the primary means of promoting special trains and services, seasonal activities, excursions and day trips. As owners and operators of a substantial fleet of ships, British Railways also encouraged all kinds of maritime activities, including non-landing cruises.

AT HARROW.

POST CARD

Prices for Delivery in BORO' of DEAL

Buy the L. & N. W. Series of Pictorial Postcards. 2d. per set of six different cards. (Over 5½ millions sold.)

(FOR ADDRESS ONLY.)

The London & North Western Railway is noted ... in the Railway Passenger Business.

	Per Ton.
BEST SELECTED HOUSE (from the best Pits)	31/-
,, SECONDS (a good House Coal)	30/-
,, KITCHEN (a useful all-round Coal)	28/-
,, NUTS (a good hot burning Coal)	27/-
STOVE COBBLES—CASH WITH ORDER (Suitable for Kitcheners)	27/6
BRIQUETTES, per 100	3/6
FIREWOOD, per 100 Bundles	5/6
COKE, per Chaldron	10/6

Discount for Cash.
Special reductions for 3 Tons & upward.
Weight Guaranteed.

The Old Established Business!
R. PEMBROOK,
(Late A. E. RALPH),
. . Wholesale and Retail . .
Coal, Coke, & Corn Merchant,
DEAL & WALMER.
Head Office—8, Queen St., DEAL.

ORDER OFFICES:
Napier Terrace, West Street, Deal.
The Coal Depot at Deal Railway Station.
13, The Strand, Walmer.
Taunton House, Cornwall Rd., Walmer.

Grove Ferry TO CANNON STREET.

RAILWAY POSTCARDS

1. Classic view of Brighton's 1880s station posted in 1907

2. 1908 card of the LB&SCR's London Victoria station

3. Card showing London's Cannon Street station c.1920

4. Card posted in 1907 showing the LB&SCR's Tunbridge Wells station

5. Edwardian card showing the Shakespeare Cliff tunnels at Dover

6. 1902 card of the newly opened Great Central Hotel in Marylebone, London

7. Edwardian view of the LSWR's works at Eastleigh

8. SE&CR 'official card' c.1910 showing Bexhill

9. SE&CR 'official card' c.1910 showing Hastings

Brighton Station, Tunbridge Wells

4

Shakespeare Cliff, Dover

5

Hotel Great Central
London W.

Monday
night 490.

Dear Mr Rebel.

Have just
arrived now
and am
in good
health
Weather
very cold
& Snow.

Rather rough crossing — Have thought about you
in the train from Newhaven — Hope you are well
Kind regards from Yours sincerely W March

6

Loco Works, Eastleigh.

7

BEXHILL STATION-DEPARTURE PLATFORM.
SOUTH EASTERN & CHATHAM RAILWAY.

8

HASTINGS STATION-DEPARTURE PLATFORM.
SOUTH EASTERN & CHATHAM RY.

9

STAFF

THE TAKING of photographs of railway employees, for record-keeping or publicity purposes, has been going on for 150 years, and this archive documents railway history in a formal manner. However, even more interesting, and more accessible, is the vast number of photographs taken informally or casually by enthusiasts and fellow employees. They have an immediacy that is very appealing and often offer a more direct insight into the working life of the railways. Sadly, few subjects or photographers can be identified.

◄ This picture of a British Railways locomotive crew resting in their cab was quickly taken by a photographer who had scrambled onto the coal in the tender. He has obscured part of the fireman's face, and neither of the men is looking particularly friendly, perhaps resenting this intrusion into what was always a rather private space. Nevertheless, it is a classic cab view, full of detail. It probably dates from the 1950s.

▲ Another 1950s photograph, this time of a crew in conversation, dwarfed by the locomotive tender standing outside their shed. Absorbed in their discussion of rosters or the day's duties, the men are ignoring, or are even unaware of, the photographer.

► In this case driver, fireman and shunter have been happy to pose by their locomotive, an old Class 4F 0-6-0, while they take a break from shunting duties. The locomotive crew look relaxed and happy, and the shunter holds his shunting pole rather formally and with a sense of pride. The date is the 1950s, and the place is a goods yard in the North or East of England.

▲ This is a fine example of a formal railway portrait, taken in about 1900. The immaculate locomotive, North British Railway's No. 9, is an 0-4-0 saddle tank built at Cowlairs in 1890 for dock or industrial shunting duties. Posed in front, and bearing their tools of office, are the driver and fireman, flanked by shunters holding their poles.

▼ Looking out of his window on a warm May day in 1982, the driver of a rather grimy and battered Class 45 diesel locomotive keeps an eye on the photographer. When this diesel was new in about 1960, he was probably still driving steam locomotives. In 1985, three years after the photograph was taken, this 'Peak' locomotive was scrapped, and the driver might well have been on the way to retirement.

◄ This moody and hastily taken picture is nevertheless highly evocative of the steam age. The driver, his hand on the regulator, keeps his eye on the road ahead. He has no time for the photographer, who, because of the cramped and difficult conditions on the footplate, might have been the fireman. Judging by cap and overalls, it is probably a 1950s scene.

◄ This group is formally posed in front of a North Staffordshire Railway tank locomotive in about 1910. In front is a stretcher and medical kit. Maybe the photograph is the record of a training session for the five railwaymen, perhaps undertaken by the two men in pale jackets, who may be doctors. Such photographs offer insights into little-known areas of railway life.

▲ In this carefully posed 1950s photograph, a neatly dressed shunter demonstrates the use of the shunter's pole. It might have been taken for publicity or educational purposes, as in the real world he would be wearing thick gloves to protect himself when handling the heavy, dirty and oily iron connectors between the wagons.

◄ In July 1965 a worn old LMS Class 5MT, No. 45014, is ready to depart from Haverthwaite. The stationmaster, or signalman, stretches up to take the single-line token hanging from the fireman's arm. This is a record of a familiar railway event, happening at that time hundreds of times each day, yet each was made unique by the relationship between the two men taking part.

▲ Formal portraits of station staff are common, particularly from the late Victorian and Edwardian periods. These men are posing on the platform at Kingscote station, on the London, Brighton & South Coast network. Their uniforms determine their status; the stationmaster is on the right.

▲ Much more informal is this group, casually posed in front of an LNER dynamometer car in Doncaster in about 1945. The group includes the locomotive crew as well as the technicians, so maybe they have just completed a test run.

◄ In a delightful image from the early 20th century, a small boy stands proudly with his father, grandfather or some other relative, in front of an old North Eastern plank wagon – a surprising choice of background for a family photograph. Perhaps it was a special occasion.

▲ Sitting awkwardly on an old chair, a Midland Railway porter clutches his dog and cat. The message on the back from Uncle Harry explains all: 'Hope in time for breakfast feeling tired after travelling all night with my little family, dont be afraid of Min she wont bite and Jimmy wont scratch I will hold them while you have a look dont kiss me Im shy.'

◄ This British Railways publicity photograph, dated 1948, is fully captioned: 'Sir Cyril Hurcomb inspects the Divisional Control Office, Manchester, which handles 2,889 trains a day. There are 268 passenger stations and 250 goods stations in the area.' Sir Cyril, later Lord Hurcomb, was the first chairman of the British Transport Commission.

▼ This classic but carefully posed photograph shows a British Railways signalman at work in a manual box, surrounded by all the traditional tools of his trade. The big wheel behind him operates the level crossing gates.

▲ In contrast to the picture on the right, this publicity photograph issued by the Westinghouse Brake & Signal Company shows the interior of a new electronic signal box, controlling the complicated track layout at Chislehurst Junction.

Staff

▼ Large numbers of men and women were employed in railway workshops, many with highly skilled trades. This 1950s view of Derby works shows a craftsman driving in firebox stays by hand – just one of the many traditional skills once used in building and maintaining steam locomotives.

▲ Another British Railways publicity photograph shows the interior of the ticket office at Southend Central in January 1957. The point was that traditional ticket offices of this kind, still in use in many parts of the network, were demanding places to work, requiring skill and patience in the selling and management of hundreds of different tickets.

▶ The modernization of the railways in the 1960s and 1970s demanded new skills and working practices. This British Railways photograph shows the electrification of a main line in the Eastern Region in the 1970s, with teams of men working from the roof of specially adapted carriages.

◀ This is a reminder that the mobile catering trolley is not a recent innovation, though this one was certainly not for on-train use. Probably taken for publicity purposes, the photograph shows two immaculately dressed LSWR catering staff with their trolley on a platform at Waterloo station. Bath buns, pies, fruit and large cups of tea are on offer to tempt waiting passengers.

▼ Surrounded by his extensive staff, a stationmaster cuts a celebratory cake, some time in the 1950s. It could be his retirement or a special birthday, but either way everyone seems happy to be included in the party. He will have to work hard to get 21 slices out of that cake!

▲ The railways looked after their staff, many of whom felt they were part of a big family. Recreational and leisure pursuits were encouraged, from sport to debating contests. The brass band was a long-established part of traditional railway life. Typical was the Midland Railway Service Messroom Band, ready for the Christmas season in 1921.

◄ Thousands of railway employees died during World War I, and many company memorials were dedicated during the 1920s, to become centres of commemoration on Armistice Day every November. In this photograph from the 1930s, a policeman adds a tribute to the wreaths piled up against the memorial to the dead of the Great Northern Railway.

WALES

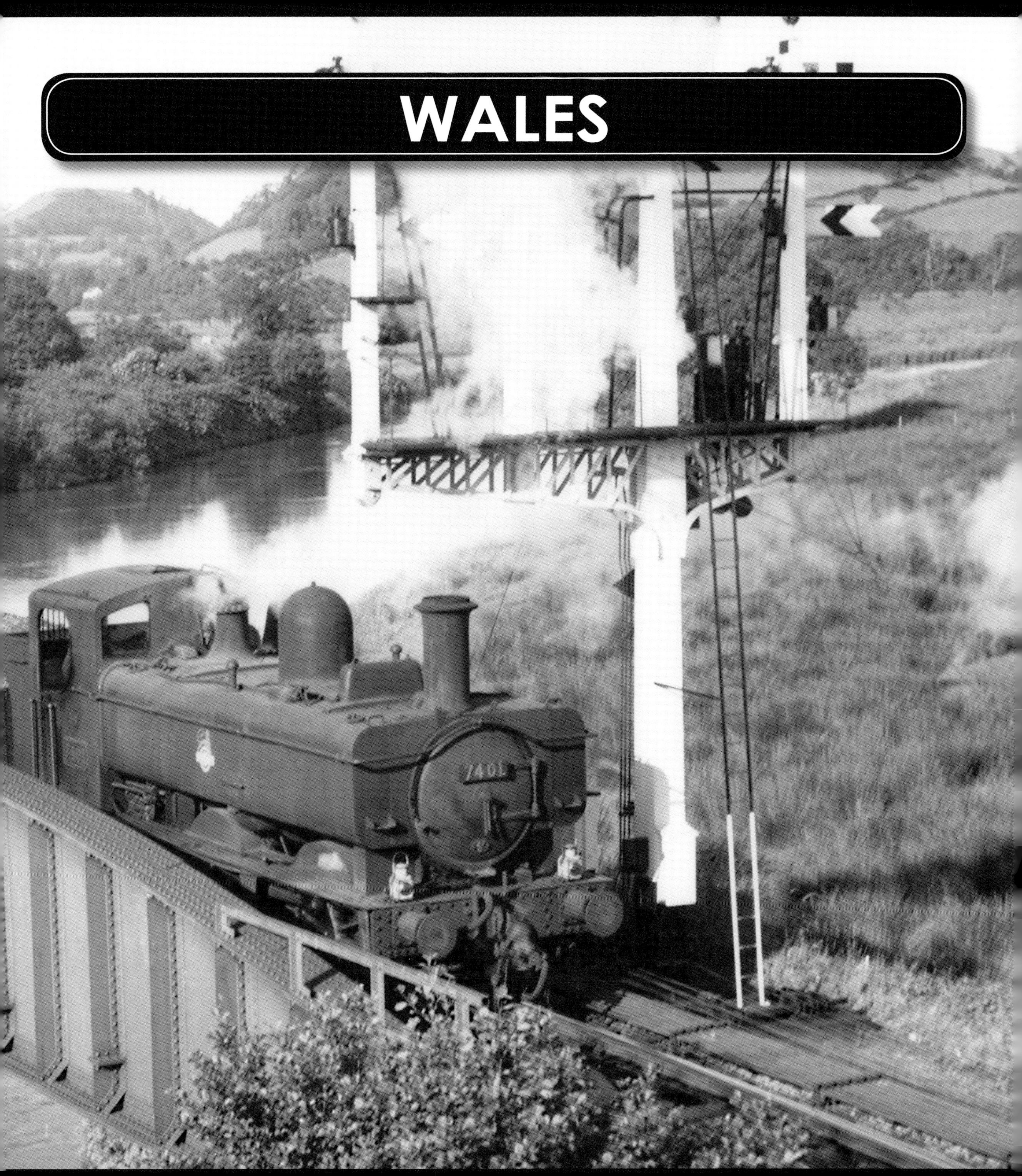

PICTURE FILE

▼ One of the many dramatic railway routes in Wales is the line from Machynlleth to Moat Lane Junction via the narrow, rock-walled Talerddig Cutting. Double heading was common. Here, in the 1950s, a former GWR Class 9000 Dukedog, No. 9018, leads the way through the cutting's twisting curves in bright sunlight.

▶ With the damp, cold weather of February 1950 keeping the smoke and steam low over the train, a suitably Welsh-named locomotive, GWR Castle Class No. 5025, 'Chirk Castle', takes a long train through Abergavenny Junction, en route to Shrewsbury and beyond.

▼ After the long haul up through the valley, the 11.15am Newport-to-Brecon local has reached the grandeur of the open hills that surround Torpantau Tunnel, and the passengers will be enjoying the view over the bare hills while GWR 5700 Class tank No. 4671 makes light work of the two-carriage train.

▼ Here another two-carriage local is hauled by a Class 2MT, No. 46401, through more splendid Welsh scenery, still looking wintry in the spring of 1962. The 12.45pm from Builth Wells to Moat Lane Junction is seen here near Marteg Halt. Such scenes were commonplace throughout the Welsh network at this time, but most were destined to change over the next few years, as lines, including this one, were closed.

Devynock Station. SJ660A.

▲ Devynock & Sennybridge station was on the Neath & Brecon line, which opened by stages in the 1860s. In 1874 it was leased by the Midland Railway, keen to gain access to Swansea. This shows a Midland train in the station in about 1910, with staff posing beside it. The station was closed in 1962, but parts of it remain. The big goods shed on the left was not demolished until 2002.

◄ In the summer of 1966 steam was still to be seen on some Welsh main lines. Here, a couple of British Railways Standard locomotives, Nos. 75014 and 76037, are worked hard as they haul a heavy holiday train from Pwllheli up the winding, single-tracked line towards Talerddig. It is a Saturday, so the train will be filled with families returning from a week at the holiday camp.

◄ This 1960 view from the cab of another GWR Class 9000 Dukedog, No. 9017, showing the rocky and winding approach to the short tunnel near Aberdovey, reveals how much of the Welsh landscape would not be seen by passengers looking out of the carriage windows on such rugged stretches of line.

▲ A familiar Welsh scene in the early 1960s, and a familiar Welsh workhorse: a Class 5700 tank, No. 9785, draws a coal train out of sidings near Cymmer, in the Rhondda Valleys.

▲ With the lions guarding the Britannia Bridge over the Menai Straits in the background, a Class 2MT 2-6-2 tank, bearing the British Railways number 41200 but still in LMS livery, takes a mixed goods, headed by two cattle trucks, from Amlwch on the Isle of Anglesey to the Welsh mainland.

▶ A local bus, a smartly dressed pedestrian and a Valleys Division train, the 11am from Barry Island to Merthyr, come together in a classic mid-1950s scene. The locomotive, a British Railways Standard Class 3 2-6-2 tank, No. 82036, has just taken the train out of Dinas Powys station.

Picture file

▶ The Great Western's Duke Class locomotives were a famous design dating back to the 1890s. A number were rebuilt later as the Earl Class, of which this, No. 3280, is an example. Many had Cornish names: 'Tregenna' was captured on film in August 1926, resting outside the shed at Oswestry.

▲ In March 1967 steam is coming to an end in Wales but there is still life in Wrexham shed as a Class 4MT, No. 76088, is prepared for the day's work.

▼ In 1958 this elderly 0-4-0 Peckett saddle tank, No. 1152, was photographed in the sidings at Swansea's East Dock. It was originally built for Powesland & Mason, who were shunting contractors in the docks from 1903. The fleet of nine locomotives were taken over by the GWR in 1924 and continued to work in the docks for many years. Four survived into British Railways ownership; this one lasted the longest, eventually being retired in 1963.

▶ In 1975 Aberbeeg was still a busy railway complex serving the local coal industry. Here, a Class 37 diesel locomotive hauls a train of empty coal hoppers back to the colliery, passing the remains of Aberbeeg station. Ten years later scenes like this were consigned to history. However, the line to Ebbw Vale, which passes Aberbeeg, was reopened to passengers in 2008.

▼ In May 1973 enthusiasts on a railtour explore the remains of Tondu station, north of Bridgend, while their DMU waits in the platform.

▲ This 1960s publicity photograph issued by the Western Region of British Railways shows a two-car DMU in scenery typical of the Central Wales line from Shrewsbury to Llanelli. The caption makes the point that this is an example of 'a government subsidised passenger train service'. This very attractive, but little-used, route was later promoted as the Heart of Wales Line.

▲ This photograph was taken in June 1977 from the cab of a DMU bound for Machynlleth as it approached the remains of Cemmes Road station. This was formerly the junction for the Dinas Mawddwy branch.

▲ In 1978 a two-car DMU waits in an almost empty platform at Llandudno, ready to depart for Manchester. At this point British Rail was reducing many cross-country and regional services to a minimum while they focused on more profitable operations, such as InterCity.

▲ In the 1990s Class 37 diesels were still common in Wales. No. 37714 was one of a group developed for heavy freight work, particularly for the steel industry. This February 1990 photograph shows it in Railfreight livery hauling a mixed freight past Cardiff Canton depot.

▲ In another view of the once-thriving coal industry of South Wales, Class 37 diesel locomotive No. 37275 takes the Maerdy line at Porth, with an empty coal train bound for Maerdy colliery.

▶ Against the classic scenery of the North Wales coast, the 11.31 Bangor-to-Crewe service approaches Abergele in the summer of 1995. The Class 37 diesel, in InterCity livery, is No. 37420, then named 'The Scottish Hosteller'.

LOST LINES

▲ *The Barmouth Junction-to-Ruabon line was a classic Welsh country railway, with a sequence of little halts that served small rural communities. Typical was Llys Halt, seen here in the early 1960s.*

I was introduced to the railways of Wales as a child and since then have been a regular visitor, travelling the lines still open and exploring some of those long closed. A favourite has always been the Cambrian Coast and the lines running inland from there, standard and narrow gauge, and several holidays have been spent in the Porthmadog area. Tracing the old GWR line from Blaenau Ffestiniog to Bala and then the cross-country route from Barmouth to Ruabon was a particular pleasure and made me wish I had taken the chance

▼ *In the 1990s, a section of the old GWR line to Blaenau Ffestiniog was kept open for trains servicing the nuclear installation at Trawsfynydd, and this gave a sense of the route in its heyday.*

▶ *South of Trawsfynydd the line was really lost. Sometimes all that remained was a low embankment across the fields, looking here much like an Iron Age earthwork.*

PANT
DOWL
EBBW VALE
NANTYGLO
BLAENAVON
(L.L.)
TYWAUN
TYLLWYN HALT

◀ A dense network of lines linked Neath and Swansea, particularly in the hills to the north. Morriston, an early planned industrial town developed by Sir John Morris to serve local metal industries, had two stations on different lines, both closed in the 1960s. This is the remains of Morriston East, photographed in 1981 with someone facing a long wait.

▲ Trains still run to Treherbert, but they used to carry on northwards to Blaenrhondda and Fernhill. In 2002 the old route was still visible.

▲ This overgrown platform is all that is left of Killay station, on the former loop line from Swansea to Gowerton via Mumbles Road. In railway terms, this was one of the more remote corners of the South Wales network. This photograph dates from 1982. Surprisingly, the platform is still there, although it is now almost buried by 30 more years' overgrowth.

▶ Three girls wearing typical 1950s skirts wait for one of the few trains scheduled to stop at Llanfalteg, the first station on the long branch from Whitland to Cardigan. The station, opened as a minor halt in 1875, was closed in 1962 and later demolished.

▲ By 1975, when this photograph was taken, Treborth station had become a private house. It still is, though today the trackbed is much more overgrown. It was on the old main line from Bangor to Caernarfon, just to the south of the Menai Bridge.

to travel it by train when it was still possible. When I first went to Llangollen, the preserved steam railway was in its infancy, and it has been interesting watching it grow and expand westwards.

Railway closures left much of Wales without railway services and for some years station buildings lingered on as a kind of memorial. A selection is shown here, including a few from the once dense network of the Valleys, a part of Wales I have yet to explore fully.

▶The Dinas Mawddwy branch from Cemmaes Road was an early closure, with passenger services ceasing in 1931. Opened in 1867, the branch had already seen a period of closure prior to GWR control. Here it is in 1951, when nature, and chickens, had taken over. The goods shed is now a woollen mill and the station is a private house.

▼ Carreghofa Halt, another minor Welsh Borders station, was on a line to the west of Llanymynech, in an area extensively developed by companies such as the Oswestry & Newtown Railway, keen to exploit local limestone quarries. The single short platform and GWR wooden shelter, seen here in the 1950s, were typical of many Welsh halts.

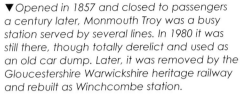

▼ Opened in 1857 and closed to passengers a century later, Monmouth Troy was a busy station served by several lines. In 1980 it was still there, though totally derelict and used as an old car dump. Later, it was removed by the Gloucestershire Warwickshire heritage railway and rebuilt as Winchcombe station.

▲ Elson Halt was on a line through the Welsh Borders from Ellesmere to Wrexham. It was closed in 1962. A couple of years later it was photographed in an overgrown state, helpfully identified by a chalked nameboard – something widely used at the time by enthusiasts.

◄ Llanwnda was a station on the line between Caernarfon and Pwllheli via Afon Wen. Closed in 1964, it was still fairly intact, and complete with signal, in 1972. Today, nothing survives and the site has been buried beneath a new roundabout.

POSTERS & EPHEMERA

▲ Wales: Travel by Train – a BR Western Region poster of the 1950s from a painting by Frank Wootton

▶ Aberystwyth: Where Holiday Fun Begins – a BR Western Region poster of 1956 from a painting by Henry Riley

▲ Colwyn Bay: The Gateway to the Welsh Rockies – an LMS poster of the 1930s from a painting by George Ayling

▶ South Wales Docks for Quick Despatch – a Docks and Inland Waterways Executive poster of 1947 for railway display from a painting by Albert J Martin

ABERYSTWYTH

WHERE HOLIDAY FUN BEGINS

Write to Publicity Manager, King's Hall, Aberystwyth

TRAVEL BY TRAIN

WESTERN REGION

▲ South Wales for Bracing Holidays – a GWR
poster of 1928 from a painting by Bruce Angrave

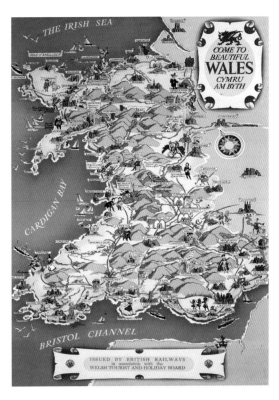

▲ Come to Beautiful Wales – a BR Western
Region poster of 1960 from a painting by
Kerry Lee

▲▼ Freight was the driving force behind the development of much of the Welsh railway network, particularly coal and mineral traffic. However, the qualities of the landscape, mountains and coastline of Wales had drawn visitors to the country in increasing numbers since the early 19th century. Railways, therefore, including small local companies such as Cambrian, were quick to encourage and exploit holiday and leisure travel. Landscape was a predictable selling point, but golf was perhaps less expected in a country not especially noted for that sport.

THE CAMBRIAN COAST

BRITISH RAILWAYS

CAMBRIAN RAILWAYS

THE GOLFING CENTRE OF WALES.

SPORTING GOLF COURSES.

HARLECH	The celebrated Royal St. David's Links. 18-hole Coast Course.
CRICCIETH	Coast Course of 18 holes.
TOWYN	Coast Course of 18 holes.
ABERDOVEY	Coast Course of 18 holes.
BORTH AND YNYSLAS	Coast Course of 18 holes.
PWLLHELI	Coast Course of 18 holes.
DYFFRYN	Coast Course of 18 holes.
NEVIN	Nevin and District Golf Club. Coast Course of 9 holes.
ABERSOCH (Near Pwllheli)	9-hole Course.
DEVIL'S BRIDGE (Near Aberystwyth)	9-hole Course.
MACHYNLLETH	Inland Course of 9 holes.
PORTMADOC AND BORTH-Y-GEST	Coast Course of 9 holes.
FAIRBOURNE	Coast Course of 9 holes.
OSWESTRY GOLF CLUB (on Llanymynech Hill.)	An Inland Course of 9 holes. (Nearest Station, PANT.)

Cheap Tickets are issued to Golfers between all Stations.

For full particulars, with Illustrated Guides, apply to

CHAS. L. CONACHER,
TRAFFIC MANAGER

OSWESTRY, June, 1910.

L. & N. W. RY.
Rhyl

PICTURESQUE WALES

ABERGLASLYN PASS (PORTMADOC STATION)

BARMOUTH ESTUARY

6D NET

CAMBRIAN RAILWAYS OFFICIAL ISSUE
Published by PHOTOCHROM Cᴼ Lᵀᴰ London & Detroit U.S.A.

6D NET

Taff Vale Railway

MOUNTAIN ASH

TO

Towyn

G. W. R.

CLYNDERWEN

Not to be used for Miscellaneous Traffic.

BARRY RAILWAY.

PARCELS WAY BILL. From CARDIFF (Riverside) to _____

No. _____ Via _____

Departure _____ o'clock Train, _____ day of _____

Waterlow & Sons Limited, Printers, Dunstable and London.

No.	Description	Name.	Destination.	Weight. lbs.	Paid on. £ s. d.	TO PAY. £ s. d.	Paid. £ s. d.	Excess Luggage. £ s. d.	Sender.
1				5					
2									
3									
4									
5									

N.B.—The Guard of the Train must see that the Entries on this Bill correspond with the Parcels delivered to and given up by him.

SOUTH WALES

RALPH MOTT

G.W.R.

FISHGUARD HARBOUR

CAMBRIAN RAILWAYS.
TO
St. ASAPH

G.W.R.

Ogilvie Halt

GWR

Drws-y-Nant to
Llanderfel

BRITISH RAILWAYS
HOLIDAY GUIDE
1956

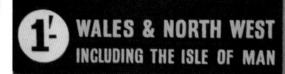

1/- WALES & NORTH WEST
INCLUDING THE ISLE OF MAN

E.R O. 48861/84

LLANDUDNO

◄▲ Many of the smaller Welsh railways were absorbed into the ever-expanding GWR, before everything became British Railways. Holidays remained a prime concern, with attractive marketing for particular areas, such as South Wales or the Cambrian Coast. By the 1950s the emphasis was on seaside resorts, notably in the annual British Railways holiday guides.

RAILWAY POSTCARDS

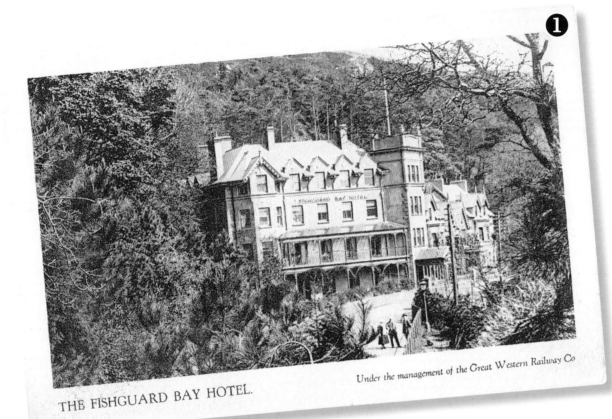

THE FISHGUARD BAY HOTEL.

Under the management of the Great Western Railway Co

❶ Fishguard Bay Hotel on a GWR 'official card' c.1910

❷ Light-hearted 1963 take on railways in Wales

❸ Edwardian view of Blaenau Ffestiniog

❹ LNWR 'official card' posted in 1914 showing Snowdon

❺ Scene near Builth Wells on an LNWR 'official card' c.1910

❻ Scene near Bala on a GWR 'official card' c.1910

❼ Classic view of Barmouth Viaduct on a card posted in 1907

❽ Card posted in 1909 showing the GWR Fishguard Boat Express

❾ 1905 view of the newly opened Vale of Rheidol narrow gauge railway

A WELSH RAILWAY

Festiniog

SNOWDON SUMMIT IN WINTER
L. & N.W. RAILWAY.

THE IRFON BRIDGE, BUILTH WELLS.
L. & N.W. RAILWAY.

ON THE TRYWERYN, BALA
GREAT WESTERN RAILWAY.

Barmouth Viaduct and Cader Idris   Valentines Series   19750

THE FISHGUARD BOAT EXPRESS TO IRELAND.
G.W.RY.

Vale of Rheidol Railway.

BRIDGES

THE CREATION of Britain's railway network required the design and construction of many thousands of bridges, the majority of which were conventional structures in stone, brick or iron. However, some posed great challenges, often because of their size or location, and the pioneering engineers of the railway age had to test their knowledge to the limit – and sometimes beyond. Great advances were made, particularly in the understanding of material technology. Disasters occurred, but many remarkable bridges survive.

◄ This photograph of the floodlit Royal Albert Bridge over the Tamar at Saltash highlights the structural brilliance of Brunel's solution to the problem of crossing a wide river 100ft above the high-tide level. Opened in 1859 after years of laborious construction at huge cost, it applied the suspension bridge principle on a hitherto inconceivable scale.

► Continental or American iron trestle viaducts were never common in Britain, but one famous survivor is Meldon. Built by the LSWR in 1874 on the edge of Dartmoor, it was enlarged in 1879, when the track was doubled. The route closed in 1968, but the bridge lived on, serving for a while as a head shunt for Meldon quarry. It now carries a cycleway.

► Brunel's response to the combined challenges of a demanding landscape and a shortage of money was the famous wooden viaduct, and he designed 52 of them, mostly in Cornwall. All were eventually replaced or rebuilt, the last one surviving until 1934. This card of the Truro Viaduct shows the distinctive structure developed by Brunel. The viaduct was rebuilt in brick in 1904, but the original stone pillars still stand.

Truro, Railway Viaduct.

▲ In the 1860s the London, Chatham & Dover Railway built a bridge across Ludgate Hill to connect Blackfriars and Holborn Viaduct stations. At the time many saw this as vandalism because it destroyed a famous view of St Paul's, as shown in this 1905 postcard sent by a French visitor to London. The bridge was removed in 1990, after the new Thameslink route was completed.

▲ The 40 brick arches of the Welwyn, or Digswell, Viaduct carry the modern East Coast main line high above the valley of the River Mimram. Designed by Joseph Cubitt and completed in 1850, it was then seen as a wonder of the railway age. This photograph shows it in 1947.

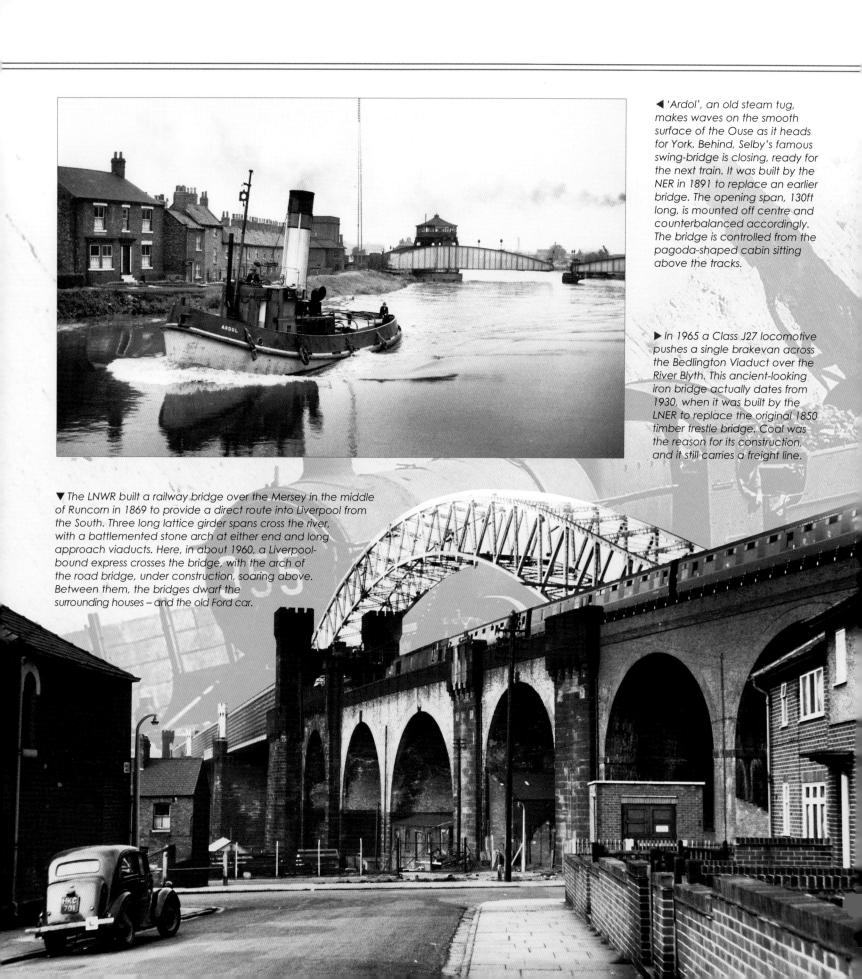

◀ 'Ardol', an old steam tug, makes waves on the smooth surface of the Ouse as it heads for York. Behind, Selby's famous swing-bridge is closing, ready for the next train. It was built by the NER in 1891 to replace an earlier bridge. The opening span, 130ft long, is mounted off centre and counterbalanced accordingly. The bridge is controlled from the pagoda-shaped cabin sitting above the tracks.

▶ In 1965 a Class J27 locomotive pushes a single brakevan across the Bedlington Viaduct over the River Blyth. This ancient-looking iron bridge actually dates from 1930, when it was built by the LNER to replace the original 1850 timber trestle bridge. Coal was the reason for its construction, and it still carries a freight line.

▼ The LNWR built a railway bridge over the Mersey in the middle of Runcorn in 1869 to provide a direct route into Liverpool from the South. Three long lattice girder spans cross the river, with a battlemented stone arch at either end and long approach viaducts. Here, in about 1960, a Liverpool-bound express crosses the bridge, with the arch of the road bridge, under construction, soaring above. Between them, the bridges dwarf the surrounding houses – and the old Ford car.

◄ At Monkwearmouth the River Wear flows through a deep gorge, crossed by a single wrought-iron, bowstring bridge 300ft long, with massive stone approach arches. Built in 1879 by the GNR, it is a dramatic structure whose severe form is relieved by the intricate patterns formed by the curved bracings. In this 1960s photograph a loaded coal train creeps over the bridge.

▼ This aerial view shows the majesty of Conwy Castle and the three famous bridges, all engineering masterpieces offering different solutions to the same challenge. Farthest from the camera is Stephenson's tubular iron bridge of 1859, showing his first use of the technique that made possible the Britannia Bridge over the Menai Straits; in the middle is Telford's suspension bridge of 1826, and nearest is the modern road bridge of 1958, with its single low arch.

THE VIADUCT NEAR LLANDOVERY ◆ A TUCK CARD

◀ This postcard view shows the curving Cynghordy Viaduct near Llandovery. The eighteen stone arches carry the single track of the Heart of Wales Line more than 100ft above the Afon Bran. The photograph shows the rough stone of the elegantly tapering piers contrasting with the smooth brick of the arches. Completed in 1868, the viaduct is still a highlight on one of Britain's best rail journeys.

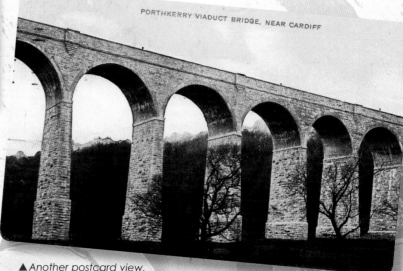

PORTHKERRY VIADUCT BRIDGE, NEAR CARDIFF

▼◀ Stephenson's masterpiece, and his most adventurous bridge in engineering terms, is Britannia Bridge, across the Menai Straits. Completed in 1850, it still looks new in the mid-Victorian photograph below, which shows the wrought-iron tubes, or box girders, through which the trains passed. The Egyptian and Greek styling, the contrasting red Runcorn sandstone and white Penmaen limestone, and the decorative details can all be clearly seen. John Thomas's stone lions, looking fierce but slightly comical, guard the entrances. The box girders were destroyed by fire in 1970 and the bridge was subsequently rebuilt to carry both road and rail.

▲ Another postcard view, this time of the Porthkerry Viaduct on the old Vale of Glamorgan line. The card is postmarked 1906 and shows the viaduct shortly after it was completed in 1897. With its sixteen stone arches, it was one of the last great viaducts to be built in Britain. The piers are notably slender, and there were problems when it first opened, with one collapsing and others having to be strengthened. It has now been reopened to passenger traffic.

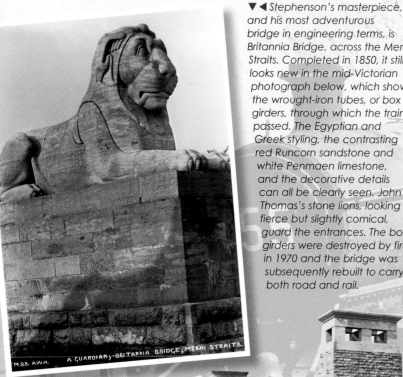

M.88. A.W.H. ◆ A GUARDIAN - BRITANNIA BRIDGE, MENAI STRAITS.

◄ The Forth Bridge is a photographer's dream, thanks to the endlessly exciting patterns created by the mass of tubes and girders that can be used to frame the trains in so many ways. This 1930s image shows 'Cock o' the North', the famous LNER Class P2 locomotive, No. 2001, crossing the bridge.

▼ This postcard, sent from St Andrews in 1910, gives a sense of the great length of the Tay Bridge, and quotes the building cost, something of perennial interest. The story of the collapse of the first Tay Bridge in 1879 is well known. This bridge, its replacement, was completed by the North British Railway in 1887 from designs by WH & C Barlow and, at just over 2 miles, it is still the longest rail bridge in Britain.

The Tay Bridge Longest Bridge in the World. Total Cost—£650,000. Length of Viaduct, 10,720 ft.

Connel Bridge, near Oban Second Longest Clear Span Railway Bridge in Europe. Total Cost, £100,000. Length of Span, 600 feet.

◄ The Connel Ferry Bridge is a remarkable structure considering it was built by the Callander & Oban Railway in 1903 to serve the minor branch line to Ballachulish. The strong currents at the Falls of Lora, at the mouth of Loch Etive, made piers in the river impossible, and a cantilever design was adopted. When built, it was the second largest steel span in Britain after the Forth Bridge. From 1913 motor vehicles could also cross, though not when trains were on the bridge. When the line was closed in 1966, it became solely a road bridge.

CENTRAL ENGLAND

PICTURE FILE

▲ A busy scene at Verney Junction during the LMS era. The date is September 1937 and the signalman watches two trains passing his box: an old Webb-designed Class 1P-A tank locomotive, No. 6699, dating from 1894, and a Class 4P, No. 1155, a 4-4-0 compound of the 1920s – a reworking of the famous Midland Railway design.

▶ It seems that in 1950 enthusiasts wandered all over the track to take their photographs. This one has found a good, if rather dangerous, place near Monument Lane station to record a Harborne special from Birmingham, headed by an old LNWR tank locomotive, a Class 1P, No. 46757. Built in 1897, this was one of 160 classmates, 43 of which made it into the British Railways era. All were scrapped in the 1950s.

▼ GWR Castle Class No. 5020, 'Trematon Castle', drifts into Woofferton Junction on a bright winter's day, probably in the late 1930s. A few passengers are waiting, including a girl proudly wearing her college scarf. The station, midway between Leominster and Ludlow, was the junction for trains on the line to Tenbury Wells and Cleobury Mortimer.

▶ Another view of a Class 4P compound, this time No. 41078, at work in the British Railways fleet. About 130 of these 1920s locomotives were still around in 1956, when this photograph was taken of the train leaving Asfordby Tunnel, on the Leicester-to-Melton Mowbray line.

▲ In October 1954, a stopping train from Ashbourne to Uttoxeter waits at a seemingly deserted Rocester station. The locomotive, Class 4MT, No. 42672, is from a group of over 600, originally a Fowler LMS design in 1927, but later adapted, first by Stanier and then again by Fairbairn in 1946.

◀ In the 1950s, trainspotters could enjoy constant passenger and freight train activity at major stations. This is Birmingham Snow Hill in July 1959, with a local freight headed by a Class 5700 tank locomotive, No. 8737, leaving the tunnel in a cloud of smoke.

Central England

▲ In May 1957, one of the ubiquitous 0-6-0 freight locomotives, in this case Class 2251, No. 2279, a Collett GWR design from 1930, heads a train of empty mineral and plank wagons down Hatton Bank.

▶ In an atmospheric scene reminiscent of *Brief Encounter,* the fireman, wreathed in steam, leans against a carriage to watch his locomotive being detached from its train. This is Wellington, Shropshire, in the 1950s, with period detail added by posters advertising Omo and a local beer.

▲ In 1962, another member of the 2251 Class, No. 2249, is busy shunting empty carriage stock at Hereford. The driver is keeping an eye on the carriages while the signalman leans out to watch the proceedings.

▶ This is Platform 5 at Leicester Central on a summer's day in 1959. Staff watch as a last passenger runs to catch the waiting train. This was a typical Great Central station, well built and well equipped with passenger facilities, as the signs indicate.

▲ At its peak, Shrewsbury was the meeting point for seven lines. Traffic diminished with the closing of three of those lines, but when this DMU was setting out in 1978, it was still a busy station. The signal box, the world's largest mechanical box, survives but is no longer in use.

▼ By the 1960s Renishaw Central had clearly seen better days. The station has closed, platforms are overgrown, and a solitary enthusiast is photographing the semi-derelict buildings. On the line between Staveley and Beighton, it had its impressive 'Central' name because another station, Eckington & Renishaw, was near by, on another line.

Central England

▼ With the driver clearly visible in the May sunshine, a Class 86 electric locomotive brings a parcels train out of Watford Tunnel. This photograph was taken in 1973, when British Rail was still heavily engaged in parcels traffic.

▲ In 1974 the mixed freight was still a familiar sight in many parts of Britain. This is the regular Bristol-to-York service passing the site of Berkeley Road South Junction, in Gloucestershire, headed by a Class 47 diesel, No. 47252. The junction had offered a link to the line to Sharpness and the old Severn Bridge.

▶ Another view in the Berkeley Junction area, this time in late March 1975, when snow was still lying on the ground. This is a Derby-to-Plymouth service, headed by a Class 45 diesel.

▲ Another 1970s photograph indicating the comprehensive nature of British Rail's freight activities at that time. Here, in June 1975, a Class 25 diesel, No. 25289, passes the remains of Cradley station, near Stourbridge, with a traditional pick-up freight.

▶ Still in the 1970s, but representing British Rail's future, rather than the past, and looking fast, clean and modern, an HST 125 in original InterCity 125 livery races through Sandy station, soon after their introduction on to the East Coast main line in 1977.

LOST LINES

I n the 1960s serious railway enthusiasts spent their time racing round Britain photographing lines and stations that were about to close, or had already closed. Others joined the numerous special trains, mostly organized by enthusiasts, that visited these lines while they still could. Some closures passed almost unnoticed, while others drew the crowds and the reporters. Sadly, I largely missed

▶ A few young enthusiasts have clustered round the cab of the old Southern Railway U Class locomotive before departure.

▼ On 9 September 1961 the 9.24am leaves Swindon Town for Cheltenham. This was the last northbound service on the M&SWJ's Southampton-to-Cheltenham route.

▲ A Great Western locomotive and Midland coaches were a typical mix on the M&SWJ line. Here, water is taken for the last time.

M 24638

▼ The last southbound train from Cheltenham draws into Swindon Town at 3.15pm, on 9 September, headed by a U Class, No. 31791.

◀ At 3.19pm the last train to travel the whole route leaves Swindon Town for Southampton. Enthusiasts lean from the windows but only one photographer, other than Geoff, has strayed onto the track.

▼ Not many have come to see the end of this particular chapter in railway history. In 1961 such things aroused little attention. Later, many closures were fought over, with good press coverage.

out on marking these momentous events, closures whose social impact was barely considered at the time. I even missed the end of my local line, the Westerham branch, in October 1961 because I was away at boarding school.

Fortunately, plenty of enthusiasts did make the effort, taking photographs to document these sad days. Typical was Geoff King, who lived in Swindon from 1958. One of his local lines was the old Midland & South Western Junction route from Cheltenham to Southampton,

▲ With a wreath more or less obscuring its number, a GWR locomotive heads the last southbound train to Andover, the 5.55pm from Swindon Town, on 10 September 1961.

◄ Earlier in 1961 Geoff King visited and photographed stations along the route. This is South Cerney.

► By 1962 trains were a memory, and the track and platforms at Ogbourne were overgrown.

▼ A Southampton-bound train pauses at Cricklade. This station is now alive again on a preserved line.

CHISELDON

▲ An unidentified tank locomotive pulls into a deserted Chiseldon station.

completed after a lot of effort in 1894. This was a typical cross-country route, relying on its many connections with other lines to win both passenger and, more important, freight business. Neither of these materialized, apart from heavy military traffic during both world wars, so the 1950s were a period of decline for a route that no one really needed. Closure came in September 1961, making the M&SWJR one of the longer lines to be lost prior to Dr Beeching's report.

Geoff King was there to take these evocative photographs of the last days. His efforts were limited to the Cricklade, Swindon Town and Marlborough area as his only means of transport at that time was a bicycle.

POSTERS & EPHEMERA

LMS STAFFORDSHIRE POTTERIES
BY
NORMAN WILKINSON, R.I.

▲ Staffordshire Potteries – an
LMS poster of 1925 from a
painting by Norman Wilkinson

▼ This England of Ours:
Oxford – a GWR poster
of 1935 from a painting
by Claude Buckle

Lincolnshire
SEE BRITAIN BY TRAIN

'THIS ENGLAND OF OURS'
GWR OXFORD GWR

▶ Shropshire: Travel by Rail – a BR Western Region poster of the mid-1950s from a painting by Frank Sherwin

◀ Lincolnshire: See Britain by Train – a BR Eastern Region poster of 1960 from a design by Tom Eckersley

▼ England's Greatest Poet – a GCR poster of about 1910 (artist unknown)

SHROPSHIRE

Travel by Rail   BRITISH RAILWAYS

ENGLAND'S GREATEST POET

GREAT CENTRAL RAILWAY SHORTEST & QUICKEST ROUTE TO STRATFORD ON AVON

SAM FAY GENERAL MANAGER

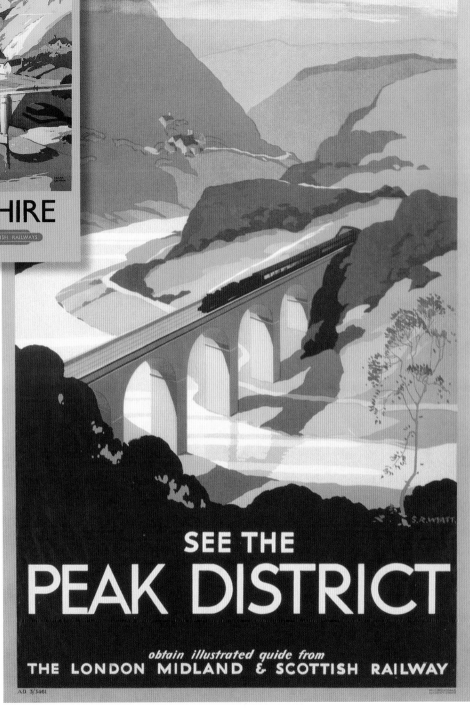

SEE THE PEAK DISTRICT

obtain illustrated guide from
THE LONDON MIDLAND & SCOTTISH RAILWAY

▲ See the Peak District: an LMS poster of the 1920s from a painting by SR Wyatt

MIDLAND RAILWAY. A. B. 7.

This ticket is issued subject to the published conditions and arrangements of the Company, and on the condition that they incur no liability in respect of any loss whatever that may be sustained by any passenger beyond the amount limited by the Merchant Shipping Acts, nor for any loss whatever caused by perils of the sea or weather.

FOR SOLDIERS, SAILORS, POLICE, &c.

No. 76   Aug 27th 1887

From Hay to Hereford Co.

Via

Officers	1st Class. Rate
" Wives	1st
" Children	1st
Soldiers or Naval Seamen	3rd
" Wives	3rd
" Children	1st
Volunteers	3rd
Police	3rd
Prison Official	3rd
Prisoners	3rd
Merchant Seamen	3rd
Shipwrk'd Mariners	3rd

Total No.   Miles   Total £

No. of Warrant

Not available by Irish or Limited Scotch Mail Trains unless stated in the Time Tables and notices to be so. Through tickets in cases where the journey the cost of transfer between Railway Termini in town required.

1005/11 1,000 2/42

CHESHIRE LINES. 186

URGENT--Perishables

Date .... 194...

From Birkenhead (Shore Road Station)

To ....

Via Helsby & Godley

TOTAL NUMBER OF SHEETS

IN or ON Wagon ....

Owner and No. of Wagon ....

Consignee ....

GREAT WESTERN RAILWAY. (3141)

STATION TRUCK.

From ....

Destination ....

Route via ....

CONTAINS GOODS FOR STATIONS

Between .... and ....

Truck No. ....

Train .... Date ....

BRITISH RAILWAYS SOUTHERN REGION BR.21764/13

TO ....

L.M. REGION

& St. Pancras

via ....

BRITISH RAILWAYS

M115

TRAIN SERVICE ALTERATIONS

LONDON (Marylebone)

RUGBY   LEICESTER

NOTTINGHAM

and

SHEFFIELD

SUNDAYS
10th and 17th NOVEMBER 1957

In consequence of engineering work between Calvert and Finmere and Woodford Halse and Rugby and between Kirkby Bentinck and Tibshelf Town on the above dates the advertised train service between London (Marylebone), Woodford Halse, Rugby (Central), Leicester (Central), Nottingham (Victoria) and Sheffield (Victoria) will be suspended and a revised service will operate as shown herein.

TICKET AVAILABILITY

Passengers holding tickets valid for travel between Woodford Halse and south thereof, and Rugby and beyond or to or from intermediate stations may travel by the train or omnibus services operating between Calvert and Finmere and between Woodford Halse and Rugby and Kirkby Bentinck and Tibshelf Town and/or travel by any alternative rail route including via London without additional charge.

PASSENGERS ARE ADVISED TO MAKE USE OF ALTERNATIVE RAIL ROUTES WHERE AVAILABLE

THE MIDLANDS HOLIDAY EXP

Will Run
from

WOLVERHAMPTON (Low Level), BILSTON (Central), WEDNESBURY (Central), WEST BROMWICH, and BIRMINGHAM (Snow Hill)

FIRST WEEK	**SECOND WEE**
MONDAY, 31st JULY TO THURSDAY, 3rd AUGUST	TUESDAY, 8th AUGU TO FRIDAY, 11th AUGUS
MONDAY - - - WESTON-super-MARE	TUESDAY - - - - - TO
TUESDAY - - - WINDSOR & RIVER THAMES CRUISE	WEDNESDAY - LLANGOLLEN & T
WEDNESDAY - LLANGOLLEN & TOUR	THURSDAY - - - - LONDON & T
THURSDAY - - - - - - BLACKPOOL	FRIDAY - PORTSMOUTH & SOUTH

FOUR DAYS' TRAVEL

INCLUSIVE FARE **80/-** EACH WEEK

YOUR SEAT RESERVED IN A SPECIAL CAFETERIA CAR TRAIN TO A DIFFERENT RESORT EACH DAY.

PASSENGERS MUST BOOK IN ADVANCE

BRITISH RAILWAYS   B.H.69

G.W.R.

Birmingham

(Snow Hill)

(18)

Great Northern Railway

TO

Nottingham

(LONDON ROAD)

▲▶ The density of the railway network in the centre of England reflects its development by a large number of competing companies. The demands of varied freight and regular passenger traffic were the driving force through the Victorian period, and these remained important in the 20th century, as surviving paperwork indicates. Typical are the documents shown here relating to the movement of soldiers, food and station supplies, and engineering works, illustrating both the complexity of railway bureaucracy and the all-encompassing nature of the railway system at its peak.

▲▼▶The development of this region as a destination for leisure and holidays began much later than in other parts of the country, and was driven primarily by its history, architecture and landscape. Shown here are leaflets reflecting all three. The LMS, and to a lesser extent the LNER, played their part, but the emphasis tended to be on excursions and short trips, many of which were determined by the industrial Wakes Weeks and similar fixed holidays. The Midlands Holiday Express leaflet, opposite, is an example of this. This pattern of activity was maintained and further developed by British Railways, who continued to promote local tourism until the 1990s.

London and South Western Ry.
TO
CHELTENHAM
Via TEMPLECOMBE and BATH.
787

Cancelling handbill L163/R HD

L266/R (HD)

Rambles in the Peak District National Park

**cheap trips to Matlock Bath
Matlock Bakewell
Miller's Dale and Buxton**

Every Sunday

15th September to 20th October 1963 and
29th March to 14th June 1964

FROM	TIMES OF DEPARTURE	RETURN FARES Second Class				
		Matlock Bath	Matlock	Bakewell	Miller's Dale	Buxton
	am	s d	s d	s d	s d	s d
...d	9 0	8/9	8/9	10/6	11/6	12/-
...	9 7	8/-	8/-	10/-	11/3	11/9
QUORN ...	9 12	7/6	9/-	10/-	10/9	10/9
...land	9 16	7/3	7/3	8/6	9/9	10/6
	9 22	6/9	6/9	8/-	9/3	10/-
	am	am	am	am	am
SAME DAY ...	11 2	11 7	11 20	11 31	11 43
	pm	pm	pm	pm	pm
	7 55	7 51	7 29	7 29	7 20

...nd 10.12 pm, Barrow-on-Soar and Quorn 10.17 pm,
...0.26 pm and Leicester London Road 10.34 pm.
...r Trent in each direction going forward at 10.4 am on outward
...n return journey.
...free; 3 years and under 14, half-fares (fractions of 1d. reckoned as 1d.).
...in advance at Stations and Official Railway Agents
...d on application to Stations, Official Railway Agents or to the
...Leicester. Telephone 23841, Extn. 34.

Remember the Country Code — Shut all Gates

1 DEC 1963

The SHAKESPEARE COUNTRY

LONDON

DISCOVER
THE BEAUTY OF THE
Buxton Spa Line
on Britain's Scenic Railway

HOTEL

UNTIL 2... ...5 1988

Supported by the
Countyside COMMISSION

INCLUDES SUGGESTED WALKS

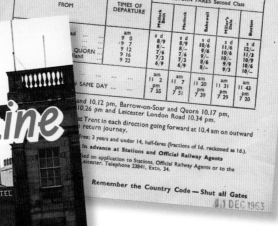

G. W. R.
BUXTON

(M 899) L. & N.W.R.
Oxford
From

ADULT AA 033827
POPE JOHN PAUL II BRITISH VISIT 1982
30 MAY 1982
AVAILABLE FOR TRAVEL FROM ANYWHERE
WITHIN THE WEST MIDLANDS COUNTY
AND ON SPECIAL BUS SERVICES TO THE
PAPAL BUS TERMINUS

RAILWAY POSTCARDS

At Monsal Dale

❶ Card posted in 1912 showing Monsal Dale and the viaduct

❷ Edwardian card of an MR 4-4-0

❸ Card showing London Road, Leicester, and the 1895 MR station c.1950

❹ NSR 'official card' of the Manifold Valley c.1910

❺ NSR 'official card' of Rudyard Lake c.1910

❻ Edwardian card of a GCR 4-6-2

❼ LNWR 'official card' posted in 1907 of Queen's & North Western Hotel, Birmingham

❽ NSR 'official card' of Mow Cop c.1910

❾ MR 'official card' of Haddon Hall c.1910

Midland Express Engine

LONDON ROAD, LEICESTER

④

WETTON MILL BRIDGE, MANIFOLD VALLEY.
(North Stafford Railway)

⑤

Sunset over Rudyard Lake, North Stafford Railway.

⑥

GREAT CENTRAL 165

⑦

QUEENS & NORTH WESTERN HOTEL, BIRMINGHAM.
ADJOINING NEW ST STATION. L. & N.W. RAILWAY.

⑧

MOW COP.
(North Stafford Railway)

⑨

HADDON HALL
WHERE ELIZABETHS BEDCHAMBER
MIDLAND ROUTE.
LIVERPOOL, MANCHESTER & LONDON.

PEOPLE

TRAINS, TRACKS, stations, buildings, signals and timetables are conventionally thought of as the backbone of railway history, but those bones remain very bare without people. Luckily, professional and amateur photographers have, since the early days of train travel, documented people – staff and passengers, men, women and children – and their railway lives and activities. Often unappreciated by enthusiasts, these images offer a rich and varied insight into the story of Britain's railways. Many are snapshots in time, featuring unidentified people and events.

◄ These young men stand and chat on a brick-paved platform somewhere on the LNWR network, possibly on their way to a sporting event. It is the Edwardian era and they look well dressed, most wearing caps and some in laced boots. The stationmaster stands with his back to them, ignoring their jokes and comments.

► During World War I, a group poses on the platform of Meir station, on the North Staffordshire Railway's network. They are mostly women, two of whom are in railway uniform. The caption on the back of the photograph reveals that one of the men is Stationmaster Walters and one of the women is his wife.

▲ This 1850s carte-de-visite photograph, taken by W&D Downey, photographers in Eldon Square, Newcastle-on-Tyne, shows George Robert Stephenson, a nephew of the great George Stephenson and also a railway engineer. In the 1860s he worked in New Zealand and was later President of the Royal Institution of Engineers.

▲ On a summer's evening in 1958 a group of workmen, looking cheerful at the end of their shift, are cable-hauled up out of the great Delabole slate quarry, in North Cornwall, on a special stepped wagon.

◀ In a classic, hastily taken snapshot, probably during the 1920s, a couple with four children look out of their First Class compartment. They are smiling at the camera, perhaps setting off on a holiday or saying farewell to relatives at the end of a visit.

▲ By contrast, this 1910 photograph of a couple looking as if they are on their honeymoon was in fact a carefully posed shot of a famous D'Oyly Carte actor, Walter Passmore, and his actress wife, Agnes Fraser. The couple used it for publicity purposes.

▶ This rather extraordinary photograph appears to show a GWR float at a local carnival in the 1930s. The theme seems to be the universal appeal of rail travel, for the group includes a sailor, perhaps going to Plymouth, a bookie en route to Newbury, a smart lady with a bouquet going to Torquay, a hiker aiming for Haytor via Bovey, and a prisoner being escorted to Princetown, for Dartmoor prison.

▼ Mossley station, north of Manchester, is a rather bleak place, set in a rocky cutting. However, in June 1982, it was a scene of some excitement as a group of cubs and scouts board a special three-car DMU taking them to Blackpool for the day. Low platforms mean a big step up into the train for the children, clustered by the door. Meanwhile, parents watch from a distance, keeping out of the way.

People

▶ A passenger, wearing a three-piece suit and perhaps posing for his companion, looks through the window of his Pullman car into the misty railway world outside. He has eaten some of his bread roll but doesn't seem to have started on his soup. The table lamp is a timeless Pullman classic, but other details suggest a 1960s date.

▼ The waiting room in Pilning station is the setting for this strangely detached 1950s family scene. The traditional table is well supplied with reading matter, and there is a pretty vase of flowers in the middle. The mother reads a magazine while casually holding their dog's lead. Her husband, equipped with binoculars, stands to read a pamphlet, while the two boys keep to themselves, one presumably playing on the floor with the dog and the other turned away in the corner.

▲ In the 1950s, a group of children await the arrival of a train at Horncastle, Lincolnshire. Some have towels and one has a camera, so they are probably going to Skegness for a day by the sea. They sit, with legs dangling over the platform edge, and one, looking slightly uneasy, has climbed down onto the track. Their position, which would be severely frowned upon today, has probably been encouraged by the photographer to make an interesting shot. One mother appears to be pulling her child away from the edge, while various other adults stand back, keeping their distance. Like so many railway station photographs, it is 'a moment in time'.

▶ A station is often a crowded place, filled with the turmoil of travel, but even big stations have their quiet moments. A photographer picked this moment at Bath Spa in 1972.

113.

▲ A huge crowd throngs the platform at Manchester's Exchange station in the Edwardian era, waiting to board an excursion train that will take them on a day trip to Blackpool. There is a sense of excitement and anticipation, and everyone has dressed for the occasion – hats are almost universal. Many people are watching the photographer, who could be standing on the carriage roof. During the season, Blackpool's stations received a constant stream of similar excursions from Liverpool, Manchester and other Lancashire industrial cities and towns.

Two visitors in plus-fours – quite possibly enthusiasts – pose at Ramsey, on the Isle of Man, in the 1920s. The locomotive is the original No.1, 'Sutherland', built by Beyer Peacock for the opening of the Isle of Man Railway on 1 July 1873 and remaining a stalwart of the railway until retirement in 1964. Steamed again briefly in the 1970s, 'Sutherland' survives, but is in store.

▼ In June 1994 a local train pauses at Grangetown, a stop near Cardiff. A couple of young women lead their children briskly towards the exit, maybe going to or from school or to the shops, or just on an outing. The train waits to depart.

◀ Another busy platform scene: this is Swindon in May 1965, and the crowds have turned out to welcome a steam special from the Midlands, organized by the Railway Correspondence and Travel Society. There are plenty of enthusiasts to be seen, but the crowd is wonderfully mixed and women and children are sharing the excitement. As ever, the people in the foreground are looking at the photographer rather than the locomotive, an LNER A3, the 'Flying Scotsman', owned by Alan Pegler. At this point, as a result of the closure programme and the anticipated end of British Railways steam, steam-hauled specials were becoming increasingly popular all over the network.

COMIC POSTCARDS

The cards on this page explore the kissing-in-the-train theme, inspired in Victorian times by the novelty of men and women travelling unchaperoned in a locked compartment. The centre card below is a later variant, dated 1929. On the opposite page are two Welsh classics – one Edwardian (top left) and one from the 1960s (top right), three cards featuring unsuitable travelling companions and misunderstandings about class – always a British favourite, and (bottom right) a 1937 example about women drivers – another common theme.

THE ROLE OF COMEDY in the history of the postcard is particularly important in Britain, where there is a long tradition of humour based on puns, bad jokes and double entendres. For postcard designers, the railways provided a rich seam of ideas, notably during the Edwardian era and the 1920s. There are many themes, but some appear perennially: fat ladies with ineffectual husbands, misunderstood instructions, overcrowded trains, screaming children and unsuitable luggage, difficulties with the Welsh language and – an Edwardian favourite – kissing in the compartment.

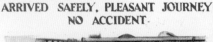

TOURIST: "Hurry up with that Label, porter!"
WELSH PORTER: "Dear Anwyl! I was thinking where to put it, syr."

ASK A PORTER WHERE IT'S GOING, FATHEAD, OR WE'LL BE HERE ALL DAY!

RAIL COURTESY.
GUARD—"Now, then, Missis, are you first-class?"
PASSENGER—"Purty middlin', thank ye. How's yourself?"

"IN THE GOOD OLD SUMMER TIME"

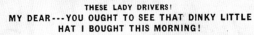

THESE LADY DRIVERS!
MY DEAR---YOU OUGHT TO SEE THAT DINKY LITTLE HAT I BOUGHT THIS MORNING!

EASTERN ENGLAND

PICTURE FILE

◄ When this immaculate locomotive was photographed at Peterborough in August 1936, it was already a veteran from an earlier generation. The NER had introduced the first of these Class V engines in 1903. The designer, Wilson Worsdell, had favoured the Atlantic configuration after a visit to the United States. Built for mainline passenger service, the locomotives were highly regarded and continued into LNER ownership. However, by the time of the photograph they were being replaced, the last survivor being scrapped in 1948.

▼ A party of ladies in elegant summer dresses and hats, one or two carrying parasols, and a few smart gentlemen wait at the GER's Thorpe-le-Soken station in Essex. It is the early 1920s, and they are probably on their way to Frinton or Walton-on-the-Naze for a day by the sea. Their train approaches but everyone, including the stationmaster and his staff, is watching the photographer. The signalman stands ready with the pouch for the single-line token.

► In a classic steam-age photograph, the LNER locomotive shows every sign of the hard work involved in lifting a heavy passenger train out of London's Liverpool Street station. Ranks of signals and Bethnal Green West signal box – about to be engulfed in smoke – add period detail.

▼ In 1951 a Thompson B1, No. 61272, that familiar workhorse of BR's Eastern Region, hauls a stopping service to Yarmouth (South Town) away from Westerfield station. It will be a leisurely but attractive journey on the East Suffolk line via Woodbridge, Wickham Market, Saxmundham, Halesworth and Beccles, with some passengers changing for Framlingham or Aldeburgh.

▲ Another B1 locomotive, No. 61043, is seen on the East Suffolk route. The setting is Woodbridge station, in about 1960. The two box vans behind the locomotive add interest and, judging by the people strolling across the footbridge, the train is in no hurry to depart.

Eastern England

▶ At its formation, British Railways inherited a massive, and highly varied, fleet of locomotives. Included were many veterans dating back to the Victorian era, some of which still had years of service ahead of them. This 1954 view of Tilbury shed shows a typical example: BR Class 2F, No. 58184, at that time, but originally a Midland Railway 0-6-0 of 1876, built by Neilson to a Johnson design.

▶ A gleaming Britannia Class locomotive, No. 70010, 'Owen Glendower', takes the 10.45am London Liverpool Street train out of Norwich station in June 1961. The Norwich shed was famous for its care of the Britannias during their last years on this route.

▲ In October 1924 a smart but apparently unnumbered and unbadged former GER 4-6-0 locomotive eases a long mixed goods train out of the loop at Trumpington, near Cambridge. A trackman, hammer on shoulder, watches it pass.

▶ Wolferton is the station that famously served Sandringham until the late 1960s. The buildings included a waiting room for the royal family and this traditionally decorative signal box. Here, in the early 1950s, one of the small group of former LNER Class D16 locomotives that survived into British Railways ownership, No. 62539, slows to collect the single-line token.

Picture file

◄ Beccles station was opened in 1859 and gradually developed into an important junction, with lines to Lowestoft and Tivetshall via the Waveney Valley. In 1969, when this photograph was taken, the island platform with its buildings and flowerbeds remains, but much of the traffic has gone.

▼ It is a wet day at Manea, between Ely and March, and in the 1960s this was an unremarkable scene. Now, the juxtaposition of a handsome signal box, wooden crossing gates and packed telegraph pole is almost unknown. The box survives, but renovated and without decoration.

▶ This is ten years earlier, and another, virtually brand new East Anglian Britannia, No. 70003, 'John Bunyan', takes a train bound for Norwich and Yarmouth down Brentwood Bank, beneath the power lines for the suburban services from Liverpool Street.

▲ By the summer of 1970, when this photograph was taken, much of BR's Eastern Region suburban network was electrified. This is Alresford station, on the Clacton line south of Colchester, a route built in the 1860s by the delightfully named Tendring Hundred Railway.

▶ In this busy 1963 scene at Bury St Edmunds a DMU waits for a platform while a freight, possibly from Whitemoor, rolls through, headed by a Class 37 diesel.

▲ Track repair and maintenance remained a largely manual activity until well into the 1950s, though machinery was in use by this time. Today, it is entirely mechanized, and this scene of a gang at work on track replacement in Essex has long been consigned to history. Indeed, the idea of using large teams of men to lift and move lengthy sections of track into place would probably be in breach of many modern Health and Safety rules.

▶ In this pre-Christmas scene in 1981, the two-car DMU for Spalding waits to depart from Peterborough. In the foreground is a BRUTE, otherwise known as British Rail Universal Trolley Equipment, a Swindon-built, parcel-handling system that was introduced in the 1960s and remained a familiar sight on platforms throughout the BR network until the end of the Red Star parcels service in the mid-1990s.

Picture file

▲ When British Railways was formed in 1948, it inherited over 9,000 horses, many of which were used for shunting. These two, shown here with their handlers at Newmarket in 1967, were the last on British Rail. Both horses retired that year.

▶ The driver of the 12.40 train for Norwich leans out of the cab of his Class 47 diesel to check the guard's 'right away' at Ipswich station. The locomotive, No. 1757, became No. 47163 soon after this October 1973 photograph. A busy life was to follow, and in 1977 it was involved in a major accident.

LOST LINES

▲ Though rather run down today, Bury St Edmunds is still an impressive station. It is a grand, Tudor-style structure, dominated by two tall, baroque towers and decorated with Dutch gables.

▶ When built in the late 1840s, Bury St Edmunds station looked like a Tudor mansion, almost eclipsing the abbey. Several lines met here beneath the great train shed, long since demolished.

Sometimes it is quite minor lines with uneventful histories that have a particular appeal. A typical example is the cross-country route from Bury St Edmunds to Long Melford. This started life as a branch from the grandly named Colchester, Stour Valley, Sudbury & Halstead Railway, later the Eastern Union Railway, whose route was opened in stages between the late 1840s and the 1860s as part of a network connecting Cambridge and Colchester.

◀ Many stations along the line conformed to a building style that reflected domestic architecture. Typical is Welnetham, seen here shortly before closure in 1961. It is now a private house.

◀ Lavenham, seen here in about 1960 and strangely deserted, had a substantial station complex, as befitted this famous medieval town. Today, only the bridge remains, surrounded by industry.

▼ A wagon piled with loaded sacks underlines the agricultural nature of much of the traffic. This is Cockfield, perhaps in the 1920s. In World War II the nearby airfield gave it a new lease of life.

▼ Today, Cockfield station and its platform survive, looking much the same as ever. All the railway details have gone, except the old VR letter box set into the wall of the bridge that carries the road over the trackbed.

In the 1960s I came to know this part of Suffolk well, though I was too late to see trains as the route had been closed in two stages: in 1961 from Bury St Edmunds to Long Melford, and in 1967 from Long Melford to Sudbury. I came across stretches of trackbed, easily spotted, and saw some stations that were still standing, including Lavenham and Long Melford.

In the early 1970s I moved away, and it was nearly 40 years before I got round to making a full exploration of the remains of this route. Rather to my surprise, this was quite easily done, with plenty still to find in the fields and woods. South of Bury, whole sections have gone, but traces remain. South from Lavenham, footpaths finally turn into something official called the Stour Valley Path, leading to Sudbury's new, very minimal station.

▼ A surviving iron bridge now carries the Stour Valley Path across the river. This is the largest of a number of bridges that remain to mark the railway's route.

▲ Only this crumbling brick arch reveals that the railway once ran through here.

◄ Passengers watch as a tank locomotive runs round its train at Long Melford in the late 1950s. Beyond is the junction, with the line to Bury St Edmunds on the right.

▼ Today Long Melford station is a smart house in red and buff brick – a suitable new life for a building whose architectural style was essentially domestic.

▲ Sudbury's station, seen here in the 1950s, was a grander version of the same style. In 1967 everything north of Sudbury was closed. This was demolished later.

▶ Today, Sudbury's basic station, with its single platform, is the terminus of a branch line from Marks Tey – all that remains of a great country network.

POSTERS & EPHEMERA

▲ Harlow Garden Village – a
GER poster of about 1920
(artist unknown)

▲ Norfolk Broads: It's Quicker by
Rail – an LNER poster of 1939
from a painting by Alison McKenzie

▲ Cromer: Gem of the Norfolk Coast – an LMS and LNER joint
poster of the mid-1930s from a painting by Walter Dexter

▼ Cambridge – a BR Eastern Region poster of 1953 from a painting by Kerry Lee

▶ Happy Holidays at Sunny Southend-on-Sea – an LMS and LNER joint poster of 1947 (artist unknown)

▼ East Coast Havens, Suffolk – a BR Eastern Region poster of the 1950s from a painting by Frank Mason

◄▼► Considering its small population and rural nature, eastern England had, until the 1960s, a good railway network. The main lines came early, driven partly by the demands of freight, notably for food and agricultural traffic, and were followed by interconnecting country routes. While the long East Anglian coastline and the many resorts encouraged the spread of holiday traffic, marketing also took care to exploit the region's history and architecture. Many named trains and expresses used the main lines, justifying the publication of lineside guides.

EVERY
and S
unti

Special

IPS

WESTERF
WOODBR
WICKH
and S

Ipswich
Westerfield
Bealings
Woodbridge
Melton
Wickham N
Saxmundham

This train will be in
train

Ordinary tickets and retu

London, September, 1928.

16762/9/28—8,000   PRINTED

HISTORY & ROMANCE IN EASTERN BRITAIN. Some Brief Tours.

BRITISH RAILWAYS
USE BLOCK LETTERS
B.R. 21233/166
19

From LOWESTOFT CENTRAL G.E.

PERISHABLE

To BISHOPSGATE

G.E. Section

Via

Letter Wagon	Number		Gross Weight	T.	C.
		3	Heaviest Lift		
Container			Crane Traffic		

*If crane power is not necessary strike out this panel.

Contents

Consignee

(18)
MIDLAND & GREAT NORTHERN RAILWAYS
JOINT COMMITTEE.
TO
GEDNEY

SOUTHERN
BRITISH RAILWAYS
REGION
Stock. 34F 3/50

TO
EASTERN REGION

Via _____ and LIVERPOOL ST.

8/50. W. & S. Ltd.

ONESDAY
RDAY

notice

te Train

ve

ICH

, BEALINGS

, MELTON

MARKET

UNDHAM

		p.m.
-	dep.	9 45
-	arr.	9 54
-	,,	10 0
-	,,	10 6
-	,,	10 12
-	,,	10 22
-	,,	10 32

at Ipswich
pool Stre——

" cheap tic——
ain.

NY'S WORKS——

G.E.R.
SP
From IPSWICH TO
GRIMSBY
via G.N. & G.E. Joint Line
and Spalding.

G.E.R.
From LIVERPOOL STREET
TO
COCKFIELD

G.E.R.
Harwich

BRITISH RAILWAYS

CONDUCTED TOURS OF

CAMBRIDGE

Every Wednesday
May 19th to September 22nd
from
KING'S CROSS

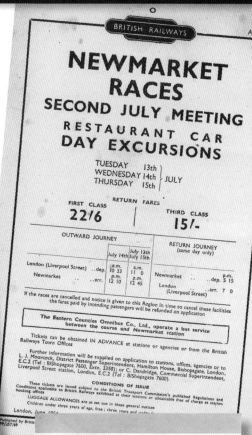

o
BRITISH RAILWAYS
A. 232

NEWMARKET RACES
SECOND JULY MEETING
RESTAURANT CAR
DAY EXCURSIONS

TUESDAY	13th	
WEDNESDAY	14th	JULY
THURSDAY	15th	

RETURN FARES

FIRST CLASS	THIRD CLASS
22/6	15/-

OUTWARD JOURNEY | RETURN JOURNEY (same day only)

	July 14th	July 13th July 15th		
	a.m.	a.m.		
London (Liverpool Street) ...dep.	10 33	11 0	Newmarket ....dep. 5 15
	p.m.	p.m.	
Newmarket ....arr.	12 10	12 45	London ....arr. 7 0
			(Liverpool Street)

If the races are cancelled and notice is given to this Region in time to cancel these facilities the fares paid by intending passengers will be refunded on application

The Eastern Counties Omnibus Co., Ltd., operate a bus service between the course and Newmarket station

Tickets can be obtained IN ADVANCE at stations or agencies or from the British Railways Town Offices

Further information will be supplied on application to stations, offices, agencies or to L. J. Moorcock, District Passenger Superintendent, Hamilton House, Bishopsgate, London, E.C.2 (Tel: BIShopsgate 7600, Extn. 2358); or C. Dandridge, Commercial Superintendent, Liverpool Street station, London, E.C.2 (Tel: BIShopsgate 7600)

CONDITIONS OF ISSUE
These tickets are issued subject to the British Transport Commission's published Regulations and Conditions applicable to British Railways exhibited at their stations or obtainable free of charge at station booking offices
LUGGAGE ALLOWANCES are as set out in these general notices
Children under three years of age, free; three years and under——

London, June 1954
Published by British——
PP/257/69

o
BRITISH RAILWAYS
A 185 (HD)

BUFFET CAR EXCURSION
TO
MANNINGTREE   IPSWICH
STOWMARKET   DISS
AND
NORWICH
SUNDAY 11th JULY

OUTWARD JOURNEY			RETURN JOURNEY (same day only)		
		a.m.			p.m.
London (Liverpool Street)	...dep.	9 39	Norwich (Thorpe) ... ...dep.		6 50
Stratford	... ...	9 50	Diss	,,	7 20
Maryland	... ...	9A 39	Stowmarket	,,	7 40
Forest Gate	... ...	9A 41	Ipswich	,,	8 0
Manor Park	... ...	9A 44	Manningtree	,,	8 25
Ilford	... ...	10 5	Colchester ... ...arr.		8 42
Seven Kings	... ...	9B 50	Chelmsford	,,	9 13
Goodmayes	... ...	9B 52	Shenfield	,,	9 35
Chadwell Heath	... ...	9B 54	Brentwood	,,	D
Romford	... ...	10 20	Harold Wood ...	,,	D
Gidea Park	... ...	10C 16	Gidea Park	,,	D
Harold Wood	... ...	10C 20	Romford	,,	9 48
Brentwood	... ...	10C 26	Chadwell Heath ...	,,	D
Shenfield	... ...	10 35	Goodmayes	,,	D
Chelmsford	... ...	10 50	Seven Kings	,,	D
Colchester	... ...	11 20	Ilford	,,	9 57
Manningtree	... ...	11 40	Manor Park	,,	D
		noon	Forest Gate	,,	D
Ipswich	... ...	12 0	Maryland	,,	D
		p.m.	Stratford	,,	10 6
Stowmarket	... ...	12 25	London (Liverpool Street)	,,	10 16
Diss	... ...	12 45			
Norwich (Thorpe)	...arr.	1 16			

A—Change at Ilford   B—Change at Romford   C—Change at Shenfield
D—Change at Shenfield and proceed by Electric Service
FOR FARES SEE OTHER SIDE

For programme of excursions from the London termini see pamphlet A 187

Tickets can be obtained IN ADVANCE at stations and agencies
Further information will be supplied on application to stations, offices, agencies or to L. J. Moorcock, District Passenger Superintendent, Hamilton House, Bishopsgate, London, E.C.2 (Tel: BIShopsgate 7600, Extn. 2358); R. E. Lawler, District Commercial Superintendent, Ipswich (Tel: Ipswich 4375); or C. Dandridge, Commercial Superintendent, Liverpool Street station, London E.C.2 (Tel: BIShopsgate 7600)

CONDITIONS OF ISSUE
These tickets are issued subject to the British Transport Commissions' published Regulations and Conditions applicable to British Railways exhibited at their stations or obtainable free of charge at station booking offices
LUGGAGE ALLOWANCES are as set out in these general notices
Children under three years of age, free; three years and under fourteen, half-fares

London, June 1954

Published by British Railways (Eastern Region)   Printed in Great Britain   Willsons, Printers, Nottingham
PP/257/23

BRITISH RAILWAYS

COMBINED RAIL AND BROADS CRUISES

RAIL AND CONDUCTED ROAD TOURS of NORFOLK COAST RESORTS

1954

◀▲▶ A range of special services and excursions were developed by the LNER, designed to appeal to shoppers, the leisure market and followers of sport. British Railways continued this tradition, making the most of the additional appeal of buffet and restaurant cars. At the same time, BR expanded into the travel business, offering package tours and outings, some combining different types of transport but generally making the railway station the starting point.

RAILWAY POSTCARDS

1. Edwardian view of an LT&SR Southend-to-London express

2. GER 'official card' posted in 1906 showing Peterborough Cathedral

3. GER 'official card' c.1910 with a view of Wroxham

4. Edwardian view of an M&GNJR Leicester express

5. GER card c.1910 showing the Cromer Express

6. The Cliffs at Southend-on-Sea shown on a GER 'official card' posted in 1906

7. GER 'official card' c.1910 showing Coltishall Lock

8. Norwich Thorpe station on a card posted in 1915

9. Edwardian view of an M&GNJR express locomotive

THE CROMER EXPRESS. G.E.R.

THE CLIFFS, SOUTHEND-ON-SEA.

COLTISHALL LOCK, NORFOLK BROADS.

Thorpe Station, Norwich

GOING ABROAD

THE DEVELOPMENT of Continental services by British companies started in the 1840s, and from that date an ever-widening choice of routes to Europe was offered on railway-operated steamers. Many services were run in association with European railway companies, and were marketed jointly; the Golden Arrow is the obvious example. Ports were also built and operated by railway companies. After nationalization,

British Railways continued to offer great diversity, along with some unusual means of travel, until the opening of the Channel Tunnel in 1994.

RAIL...

nental tables

28th May 1960 inclusive

...ices to and from

ITALY
LUXEMBOURG
POLAND
...VAKIA   PORTUGAL
ROUMANIA
SCANDINAVIA
SPAIN
SWITZERLAND
TURKEY
YUGOSLAVIA
...HANNEL ISLANDS

◀▲▼▶ This selection of publicity material promoting Continental travel ranges from the early 1900s (the postcard of Dover) to the 1980s (the three British Rail leaflets). Unusual methods of travel include the Night Ferry, the Car Sleeper Express and the Jetfoil, a very short-lived route of the late 1980s. The leaflets are aimed variously at the holidaymaker, the business traveller and the daytripper. The cover of the 1959 Continental Timetables features national stereotypes typical of that era.

Depart London 10 p.m. until 27th October, 1962 and from 31st March, 1963

London 9 pm   **Brussels 8:58 am**

LONDRES
NEWHAVEN
DIEPPE
PARIS

DE PARIS - Sᵗ - LAZARE
A
LONDRES
via
DIEPPE - NEWHAVEN
le chemin le plus court

■ Service rapide, économique, confortable

■ Excursions d'un ou deux jours à prix forfaitaires à l'occasion de certaines fêtes.

■ Billets spéciaux à prix réduits, valables 17 jours, délivrés toutes les semaines et à certaines dates.

CHEMINS de FER de L'ÉTAT et du SOUTHERN RAILWAY

◀ There were many reasons for the British to travel to Europe by train. This 1920s photograph shows a predominantly female group of pilgrims and invalids arriving at Lourdes, in the care of priests and clearly on an organized tour. The shadow of World War I must have lain heavily over such visits. The pursuit of health and religion took many people to France at this time.

▶ Between the 1880s and 1914 an extensive railway network was developed in the Landes region, between Bordeaux and Dax. Many of the lines served the timber trade, and much of the network survived into the 1950s. This shows a typical train departing from Magescq station, near Dax.

▶ In June 1963 a heavy holiday train pauses in Amiens station. At its head is a former Nord Class 231 E 5, a classic Chapelon design dating from the early 1930s. The SNCF continued to operate locomotives of this type until the end of mainline steam in France in the mid-1970s. One of the last steam-hauled routes linked Amiens with the Channel ports, so this scene would have been familiar to British holidaymakers long after mainline steam came to an end in Britain.

◀ Locomotive sheds have always appealed to the railway enthusiast, in France as in Britain. This 1948 photograph shows such a visit, in this case by Swiss and French friends to the Dépôt de la Villette, a large shed to the east of Paris, built originally to serve the Gare de l'Est.

▶ Crew and staff pose with a locomotive at Budel station in the Netherlands in about 1900. The station, serving a small village near the border, opened in 1879 and closed in 1953. Customs offices, a restaurant and other facilities made it much larger than a typical village station.

▲ The Class 50 locomotive was one of the mainstays of the German freight networks, and over 3,000 were built between 1939 and 1948. This camouflaged example, No. 50 478, was probably photographed in 1945 after it had been taken over by the 735th Railway Operating Battalion of the United States army, based initially in Coutances, France.

ECCENTRICITIES

THANKS TO their complex rules and regulations, backed up by an all-encompassing bureaucracy, railways were famous generators of notices, documents, leaflets and other assorted paperwork. Luckily, plenty survives, offering an extraordinary and often entertaining insight into the working of the railway mind and the labyrinthine, impenetrable language in which such things were often composed.

▲This painted notice, photographed in 1951, is a reminder that the Tollesbury branch line in Essex was a remote and rural railway whose operations were sometimes at odds with country pursuits.

▲Another linguistic masterpiece, this time from British Railways. One wonders how many loco workmen or other servants were 'severely noticed' for failing to obey it?

▼ Even minor accidents produced mountains of paperwork and reports. This 1957 collision form probably related to a shed incident.

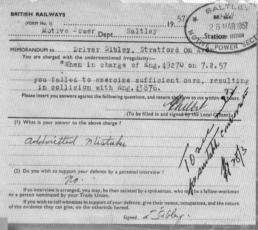

▶ The saga of Gaskell's bicycle in 1912 not only makes exciting reading but also reveals the complexity of daily railway life.

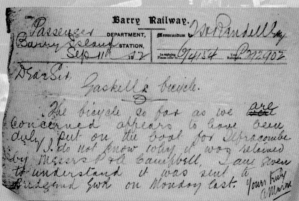

▲ The linguistic complexity of this notice at Shepherdswell, in Kent, must surely have delayed vehicles while their drivers struggled to make sense of it.

▶ This 1922 letter from the General Manager of the SE&CR shows that pulling strings and extracting favours is nothing new. Let's hope the Major enjoyed his day at the races.

GLOUCESTER STATION.   10th February 1943.

Re - Motor Car. M. G. 4040. Parked in Plaza Car Park.

I respectfully report that at 8.15.pm today I was on duty in the Plaza Car Park and saw a Motor Car Index No G. M. 4040 parked therein.

I went to examin this car and found a man and woman sitting in it. The man gave his name as Mr John TAYLOR living at 12. Llanthony Rd, GLOUCESTER.

I asked him for what reason he was useing the Car and he said " I have been to the Pictures".

I asked him for his driving Licence, Certificate of Insurance and Identity Card but he was unable to produce either so I issued him with Form P.62 and a form for him to show them at this Station, within the datum period.

I respectfully ask that the Clerk on duty - when these documents are shown- may enquire for what purpose the Car was being used, and take a Statement from him with a view to ascertaining if an offence has been committed under the "Fuel Control Order. 1942.

The Inspector on Duty.   Joseph H. Lilley

                                          P.W.R. 149.

▲ This incident report from 1943 highlights the multiple responsibilities of the railways during wartime, which included the enforcement of government traffic orders and controls. Though the couple in the car were probably doing no more than what couples often do in parked cars, John Taylor was clearly in trouble.

▲ The great diversity of freight carried by the railways also generated quantities of documents. Many were very specific, including this LNER form for the conveyance of horses for breeding purposes.

TRAVELLERS to ETERNITY

UP LINE	DOWN LINE
All who believe in the Lord Jesus Christ will be **Caught Up** to Glory, to be for ever with the Lord.	All who neglect God's Great Salvation will be **Cast Down** to Hell, with the Devil and his Angels.

WHICH LINE ARE YOU ON TO-DAY?

G.R.T. No. 7.   St. Margaret's Press, Northolt.

◀ In the Victorian era 'gospel railway tickets' were handed to passengers at railway stations by evangelical preachers.

BRITISH RAILWAYS

The Railway Executive (Eastern, London Midland, North Eastern and Scottish Regions) hereby give notice of the following revised Charges on which their Grain Sacks are let out on hire, **to take effect on and from 1st March, 1951 :—**

(a) **Sacks hired empty.**
1¼d. per sack for a period not exceeding **7 days**, including dates of hire and return.

(b) **Sacks forwarded full by Railway Executive Transport.**
A further **14 days** allowed from the date of despatch if forwarded full by Railway Executive Transport.

(c) **Sacks detained beyond the above periods—Demurrage Charges:**
1d. per sack per week, or part thereof, will be charged after the above periods.

(d) **Sacks hired (full) by Consignee or Transferee under fresh Contract.**
The charge for demurrage, as in (c), will commence when the period specified in (b) under the previous contract has expired.

Note. Sunday, Good Friday, and Christmas Day (England and Wales) or New Year's Day (Scotland), will be treated as normal days.

(e) **Stay Hire.**
A charge to stay hire of 10s. 0d. per sack in addition to other charges which may be due, will be made on sacks not returned to the Railway Executive.

◀ The hiring of grain sacks was one of many business activities taken on by railway companies, as indicated by this verbose 1951 handbill. Overall, British Railways were masters of obfuscation.

▼ ▶ This card from 1945 hints at the huge amount of correspondence that stationmasters had to undertake on a daily basis. It is a relief to know that the Fordham family's pram made it safely from north Norfolk to Oxted station, near their farm in Edenbridge in Kent.

POST CARD
THE ADDRESS TO BE WRITTEN ON THIS SIDE

The Station Master.
M. & G.N. Railway,
West Runton Station.
NORFOLK.   WEST RUNTON.

GRUBBS FARM.
Staffhurst Wood,
Nr Edenbridge.
Kent.
20.8.45.
REF. WR.649.

I am in receipt of your communication re. my pram, & now am pleased to inform you this was received at Oxted last Friday & I thank you for your trouble in this matter.
Yours truly,
C. B. Fordham.

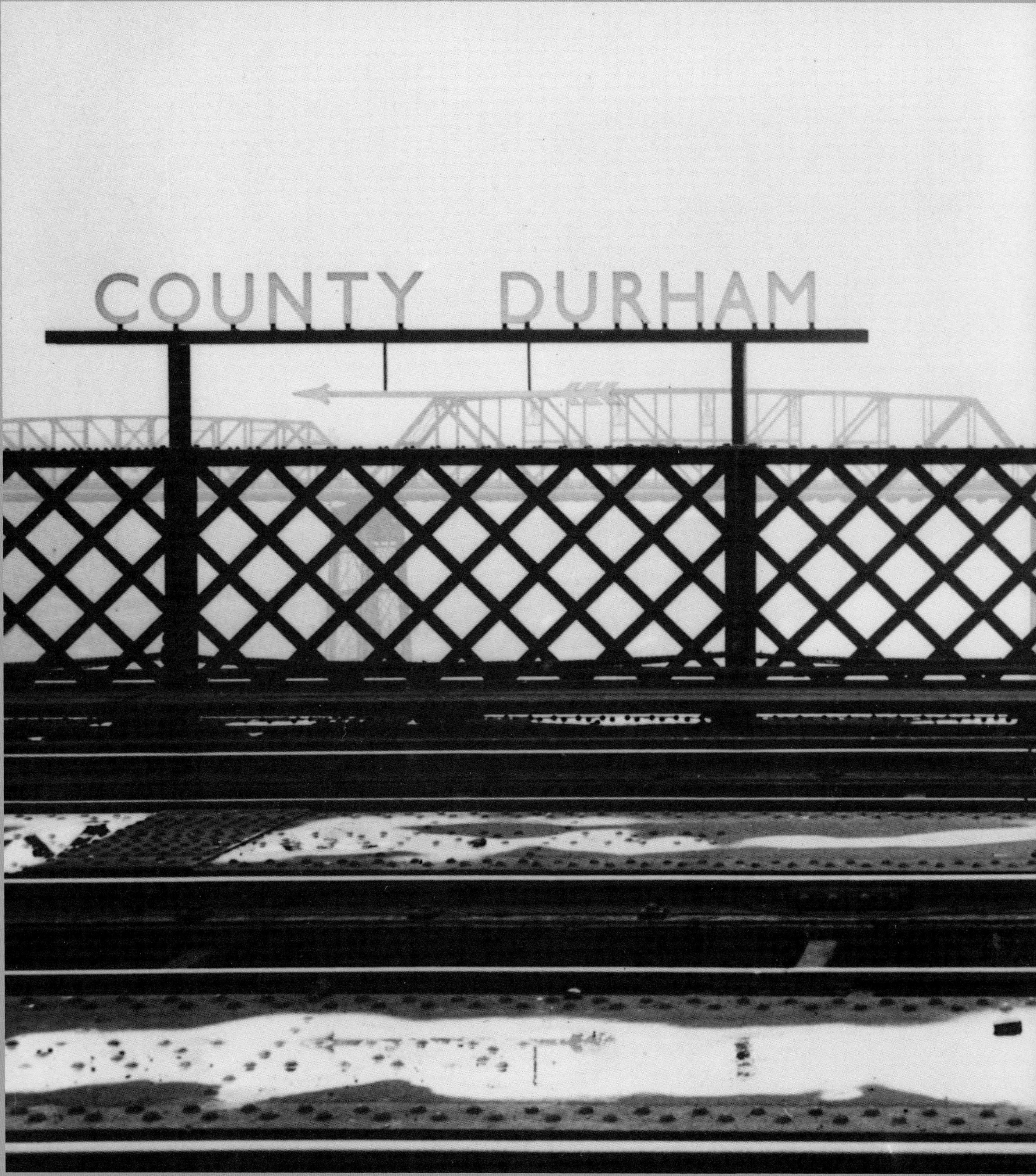
COUNTY DURHAM

PICTURE FILE

▲ Sadly, some railway enthusiasts are rather poor photographers. This out-of-focus shot of the LMS's Coronation Scot passing through Crewe station on 1 August 1939 is one example, but the result is actually exciting and, by chance, captures a sense of the speeding express and its streamlined locomotive, No. 6222, 'Queen Mary'.

▲ This somewhat better picture of the LNER's streamlined rival, Class A4 No. 60030, 'Golden Fleece', photographed exactly 22 years later, is full of enthusiast's detail in its caption. The London-to-Edinburgh express is on a diversionary route via Bishop Auckland, passing Dearness Valley signal box and, on the right, the Waterhouses branch.

▼ In a flurry of smoke and steam, a Liverpool-to-Newcastle express races out of Standedge Tunnel, piloted by a Stanier 5MT Jubilee, No. 45063. It is a classic scene from the 1960s, in a typically magnificent landscape setting.

▲ This evocative photograph shows Barnsley Exchange Junction in 1967. Sidings are full of mineral wagons and a battered-looking former LMS Class 5MT, No. 44857, ekes out its last days in shunting duties while diesels rest in the foreground.

▼ An enthusiast, precariously placed on the steep embankment, catches the moment as an elderly former LNER Class B16 locomotive, No. 61425, swings onto the York line at Micklefield, east of Leeds, with an express bound for Scarborough. The coaching stock is very mixed in this late 1950s image.

Northern England

◄ On a quiet summer's day at Carlisle in the late 1950s, a former LMS tank locomotive from the 1920s, No. 47326, takes a break from station shunting duties.

▼ At the other end of the steam spectrum, in complete contrast to the image above, this 1958 photograph of Scotsgap Junction shows the couple of wagons that made up the Morpeth-to-Rothbury goods behind an elderly Class J25 0-6-0 locomotive.

▶ Another classic view from the last years of steam: an Ivatt Class 4MT 2-6-0, No. 43004, on duty as station pilot at Preston on 29 June 1967, waits under the signal gantry.

Picture file

◀ Steam-hauled freights were a regular sight on the northern section of the West Coast main line during the early 1960s. Here, a former LMS Stanier-designed Class 5MT locomotive, No. 44670, shows its power at the head of a long mixed freight, blasting smoke across the Cumbrian landscape.

▲ This February 1947 photograph, showing a southbound passenger train marooned near Kirkby Stephen, captures the flavour of that famously terrible winter.

◀ In 1931 an exceptional freight – 625 tons of castings for the new Cunarder (later 'Queen Mary') – is inched through Hartburn Bridge in Durham.

▼ With crowds of spectators watching, an LNER passenger service, running on the wrong track, crawls past a maintenance team busily preparing to replace a bridge. The photograph is undated, but is probably from the 1930s.

Northern England

▲ A Class 40 diesel hauls a Liverpool-to-London express off the Runcorn Bridge, over the Mersey, in the early 1960s. Pedestrians stand and watch on the footbridge. This was part of the original structure but was closed after the opening of the adjacent road bridge.

◀ In hard winter sunlight in 1973, the northbound Flying Scotsman, hauled by Deltic Class diesel 'Crepello', arrives in Newcastle.

▶ In August 1971 the train is modern, but the elevated signal box, the semaphore signals and the closed line to Adlington at Boar's Head Junction, near Wigan, are all reminders of an earlier era. The Class 47 diesel, No. 1729, later No. 47137, was scrapped and cut up in 1991.

▲ By 1977 the Class 47 diesels were to be found all over the network. This example, No. 47540, was captured on the approach to Stainforth Tunnel, near Settle, with a mixed freight for Carlisle yard. Later, the locomotive carried a name, 'The Institution of Civil Engineers'.

▲ In a busy scene near Chesterfield in the 1980s, an HST 125 powers its way between two freight trains, one loaded with ballast and the other, hauled by a Class 45 diesel, with steel bars. To the right are sidings filled with loaded coal trains.

◀ In a magnificent winter setting near Threlkeld, a two-car DMU forms the 11.05 Keswick-to-Penrith on 12 February 1972. Three weeks later, on 6 March, this lovely scenic line was closed.

LOST LINES

In any Desert Island list of favourite closed railway lines, I would always include the trans-Pennine route from Darlington to Penrith, along with its extension through the Lakes to Cockermouth. This must have been one of Britain's best journeys, a spectacle of glorious but extreme landscape from start to finish. That same landscape challenged the line's builders in the 1860s and continued to challenge all those involved in running it for the next 100 years. I did not explore the route until the mid-1990s, by which time it had nearly all been closed for 30 years, but it was a great experience, mostly in a cold but clear December with snow on the high ground and plenty of memorable discoveries, some hinted at here.

▲ At 1370ft, Stainmore Summit was the highest in England. Crossing it was always a challenge, particularly in winter. When the line was closed, the iron sign that marked the summit was preserved.

▲ Belah was the most impressive of Britain's few iron trestle viaducts and a major feature of the line. It was designed by Thomas Bouch, of Tay Bridge infamy. Freight trains, the line's most regular traffic, were usually banked for the climb to the summit.

▶▼ *Things to excite explorers of lost railways are old stations hidden in woods, such as Bassenthwaite Lake (right), which closed in 1966 and is therefore an unexpected survivor. By contrast, massive embankments, like the one near Clifton (below), tend to endure and, even if overgrown, have a real railway presence.*

◀ *The last section of the line to close, in 1972, was Penrith to Keswick, by then an extended branch line. This is Threlkeld, an intermediate station, a couple of years later. Only the platform remains.*

▲ *Signal boxes are ephemeral and survive only if someone makes the effort to protect them. This one lived on after the closure of the line through Cliburn station in 1962 because the new owner of the site decided it would make a good summer house – with a view.*

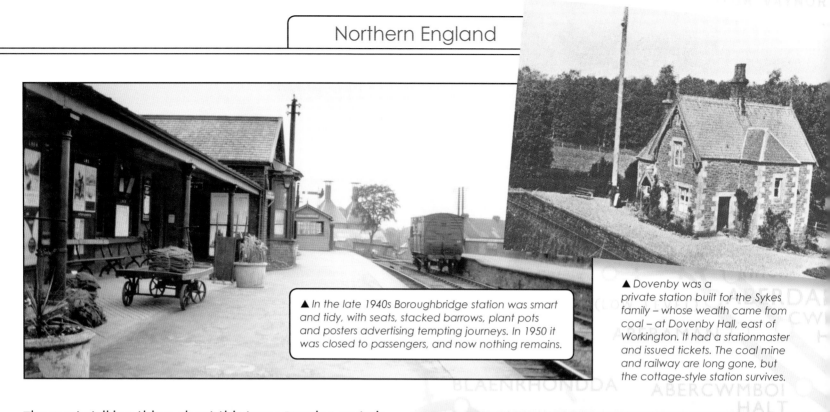

▲ In the late 1940s Boroughbridge station was smart and tidy, with seats, stacked barrows, plant pots and posters advertising tempting journeys. In 1950 it was closed to passengers, and now nothing remains.

▲ Dovenby was a private station built for the Sykes family – whose wealth came from coal – at Dovenby Hall, east of Workington. It had a stationmaster and issued tickets. The coal mine and railway are long gone, but the cottage-style station survives.

The most striking thing about this trans-Pennine route is its enduring physical presence in the landscape, survival guaranteed in this case by remoteness and lack of any subsequent change or development. When railways are closed, it is usually the infrastructure and the buildings that disappear. Stations can survive, simply because many work perfectly well as houses or can be adapted for other domestic or commercial purposes, but other structures – signal boxes, goods warehouses, engine sheds, water towers, tool stores – tend to vanish quite quickly, destroyed either by intent or by decay. Thus, one of the pleasures of exploring lost railways is finding structures, or the remains of them, hidden in the landscape, vital and living memorials to their railway past.

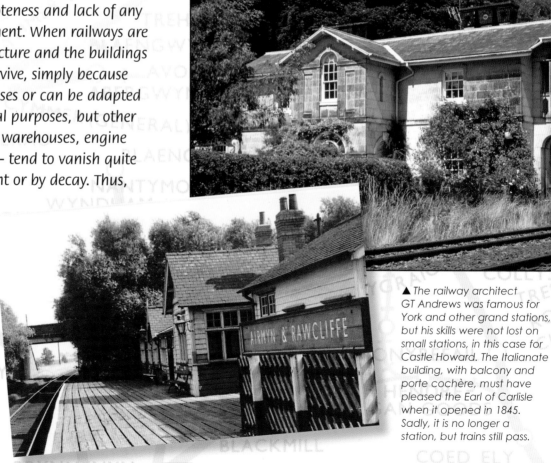

▶ Airmyn & Rawcliffe was a rural station on one of the lines radiating from Goole. A simple timber structure, it opened in 1912 to serve a growing village. By the 1960s it was little used and it closed in 1964.

▲ The railway architect GT Andrews was famous for York and other grand stations, but his skills were not lost on small stations, in this case for Castle Howard. The Italianate building, with balcony and porte cochère, must have pleased the Earl of Carlisle when it opened in 1845. Sadly, it is no longer a station, but trains still pass.

▲ The coastal line linking Scarborough and Whitby opened in 1885, and one of its features was a sequence of grand, stone-built stations serving small communities. When the line closed in 1965, several of these lived on as private houses, including Staintondale, delightfully set in woodland.

▶ A universal feature of the railway scene, now almost invariably lost, was the engine shed. Images like this early 1960s view of Hull Dairycoates (53A) have, as a result, great appeal. Here, three NER Victorian veterans by Worsdell and a Gresley LNER 0-6-0 face the turntable.

POSTERS & EPHEMERA

▲ Liverpool Overhead Railway – a Liverpool Overhead Railway poster of 1910 (artist unknown)

▲ Whitby, Yorkshire – a BR North Eastern Region poster of 1954 from a design by André Amstutz

NEW GUIDE FREE FROM INFORMATION BUREAU BRIDLINGTON OR ANY L·N·E·R INQUIRY OFFICE OR AGENC

LONDON & NORTH EASTERN RAILWAY

EXPRESS EASE

THE "HARROGATE" PULLMAN
LIMITED TRAIN
Between KING'S CROSS (London) and
LEEDS in 3½ hrs. HARROGATE 4 hrs. RIPON 4½ hrs.
Also DARLINGTON and NEWCASTLE

▲ Express Ease: The Harrogate
Pullman – an LNER poster of
1923 from a painting by
George Harrison

▲ Bridlington – an
LNER poster of 1932
from a painting by
Tom Purvis

◀ Service to Industry –
a BR North Eastern
Region poster of 1962
from a painting by
Terence Cuneo

▶ Ullswater: English
Lake-Land – an LNER
poster of 1923 from
a painting by John
Littlejohns

SERVICE TO INDUSTRY

THE GREAT I C I CHEMICAL WORKS AT BILLINGHAM-ON-TEES DEPEND
ON BRITISH RAILWAYS FOR THE DELIVERY EACH YEAR OF NEARLY TWO
MILLION TONS OF COAL, 150,000 TONS OF OTHER COMMODITIES, AND FOR
THE DISPATCH OF THREE-QUARTERS OF A MILLION TONS OF FERTILISERS,
CEMENT, BULK LIQUIDS AND OTHER PRODUCTS.

ULLSWATER ENGLISH LAKE-LAND
RAIL · MOTOR · STEAMER DAY TOURS
FROM THIS STATION
FULL PARTICULARS AND LITERATURE FROM BOOKING OFFICE

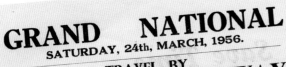

GRAND NATIONAL
SATURDAY, 24th, MARCH, 1956.
TRAVEL BY
OVERHEAD RAILWAY
WITHOUT CHANGING
DIRECT TO AINTREE RACECOURSE

		a.m.	a.m.	a.m.	p.m.	p.m.	p.m.	p.m.	p.m.	p.m.	p.m.	p.m.	p.m.	p.m.
DINGLE	dep.	11 25	11 40	12 25	12 35	1 5	1 14	1 23	1 33	1 47	1 54		
JAMES STREET		11 35	11 50	12 35	12 45	1 15	1 24	1 33	1 43	1 49	2 6		
PIER HEAD		11 37	11 52	12 37	12 47	1 17	1 26	1 35	1 45	2 8	2 23		
SEAFORTH SANDS	arr.	11 52	12 8	12 53	1 3	1 33	1 42	1 52	2 3	2 18	2 32		
AINTREE (No. 3 Platform)	arr.	12 2	12 16	1 3	1 13	1 41	1 52	2 3					
		p.m.	p.m.	p.m.	p.m.	p.m.	p.m.	p.m.	p.m.	p.m.	p.m.		
AINTREE	dep.	3 50	4 4	4 24	4 42	4 51	5 4	5 12	5 41		5 31		
SEAFORTH SANDS		4 18	4 19	4 34	4 51	5 1	5 14	5 18	5 26	5 41		
PIER HEAD		4 18	4 33	4 48	5 8	5 18	5 27	5 55				
JAMES STREET		4 19	4 34	4 49	5 9	5 19	5 28	5 56				
DINGLE	arr.	4 28	4 43	4 58	5 28	5 36						

FARES from	Single	Return
DINGLE, HERCULANEUM, TOXTETH, BRUNSWICK, WAPPING and CANNING	1/-	2/-
JAMES STREET PIER HEAD CLARENCE, NELSON HUSKISSON CANADA, BROCKLEBANK, and ALEXANDRA	10ᴰ	1/8
GLADSTONE SEAFORTH SANDS	6ᴰ	1/-

The issuing of Through Tickets is subject to the conditions and regulations referred to in the Time Tables, Bills, and Notices of the respective Companies on whose Railways, Coaches or Steamboats they are available, and the holder, by accepting a Through Ticket agrees that the respective Companies Railways to be liable for any loss or damage, injury, delay or detention caused or arising off their respective Railways, Coaches or Steamboats. The Contract and liability of each Company are limited to its own Railway, Coaches or Steamboats.

Hargreaves Building, 5, Chapel Street, Liverpool, 3. March, 1956.

H. MAXWELL ROSTRON, General Manager & Engineer.

PLEASE RETAIN FOR REFERENCE

HOLIDAY RUN-ABOUT TICKETS
LANCASHIRE COAST
THE LAKE DISTRICT
West Cumberland and Westmorland
ISSUED 30th APRIL to 28th OCTOBER 1961
SECOND CLASS

AREA No. 2	AREA No. 4	AREA No. 3
25/-	35/-	27/6
Available for 6 days commencing any day except Saturday Not issued on or valid for travel on Saturdays		Available for 7 days commencing any day

- Children of 3 and under 14 years of age half fare
- Unlimited number of journeys within the area
- Break of journey allowed at any station
- Tickets are NOT TRANSFERABLE and must be signed by the holder
- No allowance or extension of date can be granted on these tickets in consequence of there being no Sunday service in certain areas

Travel in Rail Comfort

LONDON MIDLAND

EA 25

PLEASE RETAIN THIS

SUNDAY 5TH SE
SPECIAL EXCU
MILLOM S
WHITEHA
WORKIN

LIGHT REFRESH
WILL BE SERVED ON THE SPECIAL EXCURSIO
ATTENDANTS PASSING DOWN THE

FROM	TIMES OF DEPARTURE		
	a.m.	a.m.	
Morecambe (E. Rd.)	N.B.	10·45	
Lancaster (Castle)	10-55	11-50	6
Carnforth	N.B.	12-5 p.m	6
Arnside	N.B.		5
Grange	11-25	12-15	5
Ulverston	11-40	12-45	3/
Dalton	11-50	12-55	3/
Millom	12-20 p.m	1-25	3/
Seascale	arr.		
Whitehaven (Corkickle)	12-50	1-54	
Whitehaven (Bransty)	1-18	2-21	
Workington	1-25	2-28	
	1-43	2-45	dire

RETURN ARRANGE
Passengers return same day from Workington at 7·20 p.m
7¹⁵ p.m. or 8·0 p.m., Whitehaven (Corkickle) 7·25 p
or 8·40 p.m., Millom 7·24 p.m., Millom 7824 p.m., 8·20
‡—Not for Arnside and Carnforth.

THE FOLLOWING LIGHT REFRESHMENTS W
Tea . Ham Rolls . Meat Sandwiches . Meat Pies
Crisps . Lyons' Gala Pies .
PLEASE PAY WHEN SER
Children under three years of age, free : three years an

NOTICE AS TO CONDITION
These tickets are issued subject to the British Transport
Conditions applicable to British Railways exhibited at their stations
booking offices.

TICKETS CAN BE OBTAINED IN ADVANCE AT STA

Further information will be supplied on application to Stations,
District Commercial Superintendent, Barrow-in-Furness. Telephone 33
August, 1954.
X5/Schedule.

Travel in Rail Com

BRITISH RAILWAYS

J. Wadsworth Ltd., Printers, Grange-ov

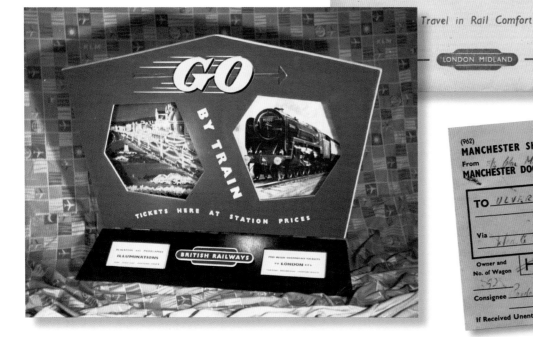

GO
BY TRAIN
TICKETS HERE AT STATION PRICES
BRITISH RAILWAYS

◄▲▼ The variety of railway paperwork is apparently endless, and most of it was designed to be ephemeral. Survival is a matter of chance, yet everything that does survive offers intriguing insights into railway history. Shown here is the usual mix of the ordinary and the extraordinary, the latter including a Liverpool Overhead Railway handbill for the Grand National and the design for a travel agent's window display panel.

(962)
MANCHESTER SHIP CANAL CO.
From
MANCHESTER DOCKS 11-6-68
TO ULVERSTON
Via
Owner and No. of Wagon H M L
Consignee
If Received Unentered Quote

BRITISH RAILWAYS
BR.21711
COACH RESERVED
For Cadets
Party
from Scarborough To York
in 8.2 a.m. Date 8 Aug Signature J. Layton

Well known – and in 1980 widely celebrated – as the birthplace of the railways, the North of England may be less familiar as a holiday region, yet its resorts, coastal regions and landscape were extensively promoted by local and national railway companies. As always, British Railways maintained and expanded this tradition. Also maintained by BR until the 1990s were famous named trains such as Flying Scotsman. Not quite so famous was The Highwayman, a short-lived named train whose existence reflected increasing competition from coaches using the new motorway networks.

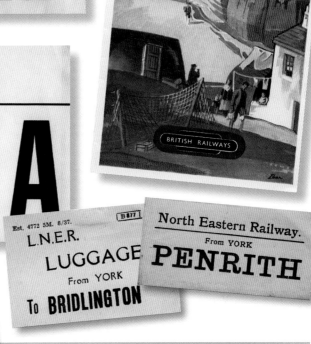

THE NORTHUMBRIAN COAST & CHEVIOTS

BRITISH RAILWAYS

B.R. 21885/202

MANCHESTER

special price
holiday travel

1971
from Harrogate, Selby and York

British Rail Eastern

THE FLYING SCOTSMAN

LONDON KING'S CROSS
via Newcastle

A

Ride with The Highwayman

The train that's 2 hours faster than the motor coach between London and the North-East and only £2·25 each way

You'll see it riding by with crossed gold pistols on every carriage. You ought to be on it.

Est. 4772 5M. 8/37. B 877
L.N.E.R.
LUGGAGE
From YORK
To BRIDLINGTON

North Eastern Railway.
From YORK
PENRITH

Monday 26 May 1980   Price £6

LIVERPOOL AND MANCHESTER RAILWAY ANNIVERSARY · 150 YEARS ·

ROCKET 150
Admission Ticket

STAND	BLOCK	ROW	SEAT
H	2	C	19

RAILWAY POSTCARDS

The River Wear and Banks, Sunderland.

1. Card posted in 1921 showing coal sidings by the River Wear

2. MR 'official card' c.1910 showing Appleby Castle

3. Durham Cathedral on a GNR 'official card' posted in 1901

4. Edwardian view of Sir Robert Walker's Sand Hutton miniature railway

5. Card from c.1910 showing the Sunderland bridges

6. Edwardian view of the Midland Hotel, Manchester

7. GNR Enterprise express in about 1920

8. Card posted in 1906 with a dramatic view of Huddersfield's Lockwood Viaduct

9. FR 'official card' c.1910 showing the Kirkstone Pass

APPLEBY CASTLE ON THE EDEN.
SETTLE & CARLISLE LINE.
MIDLAND ROUTE
BETWEEN ENGLAND & SCOTLAND.

④

⑤

SUNDERLAND BRIDGES.   Copyright. F. F. & Co.

⑥

MIDLAND HOTEL MANCHESTER

⑦

(NER) ENTERPRISE EXPRESS

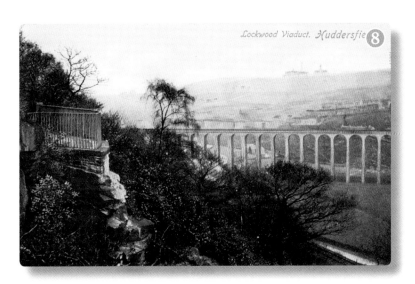

⑧

Lockwood Viaduct. Huddersfie

⑨

KIRKSTONE PASS AND BROTHERS WATER   AMBLESIDE STATION.

NARROW GAUGE

ORIGINALLY OPERATED primarily for industrial purposes, narrow gauge lines were found throughout Victorian Britain. During the late 1900s passenger carrying became more common and new lines appeared, often driven by the expansion of the leisure market. By the 1930s, however, narrow gauge was in decline and many lines closed. The survivors, famous for their diversity in gauge, locomotives, rolling stock and landscape, turned themselves into heritage steam railways. Shown here are lines in England and Wales, along with cliff railways.

◄ *The rolling stock on the Southwold Railway included a variety of passenger carriages, including six-wheelers with open verandah ends. This shows a rebuilt 1st/3rd composite carriage in about 1927, with plenty of passengers on board. There was also a fleet of freight wagons. Rolling stock and locomotives were abandoned at closure and were broken up on site years later.*

▶ *One of England's best-known narrow gauge lines was opened in 1879 to link the Suffolk seaside resort of Southwold with the Great Eastern's main line at Halesworth. The railway carried passengers, mineral traffic and general freight, and was popular with holidaymakers. There were four locomotives, built by Sharp Stewart and Manning Wardle. There were plans to expand the line, but competition from road traffic brought those to nought and in the end it was the faster motor buses that killed the line. In this photograph, taken on the day of closure, 11 April 1929, the stationmaster, Mr Girling, shakes hands with John Stannard, a long-serving driver, in front of locomotive No. 3, 'Blyth'.*

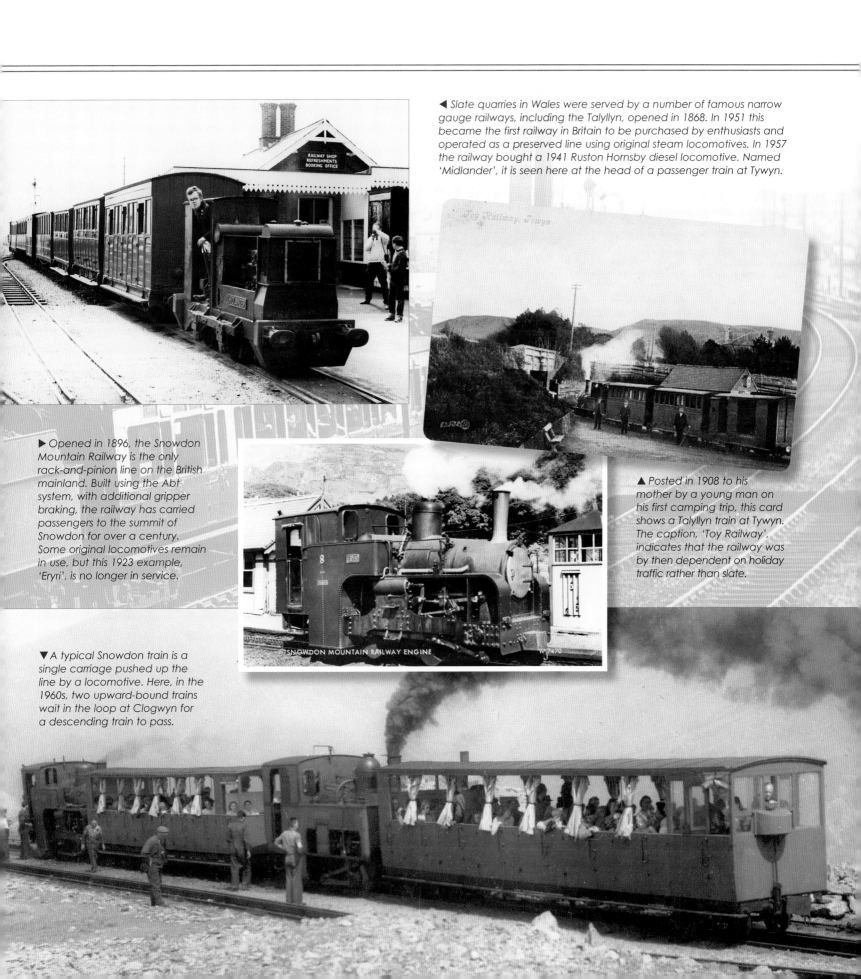

◀ Slate quarries in Wales were served by a number of famous narrow gauge railways, including the Talyllyn, opened in 1868. In 1951 this became the first railway in Britain to be purchased by enthusiasts and operated as a preserved line using original steam locomotives. In 1957 the railway bought a 1941 Ruston Hornsby diesel locomotive. Named 'Midlander', it is seen here at the head of a passenger train at Tywyn.

▶ Opened in 1896, the Snowdon Mountain Railway is the only rack-and-pinion line on the British mainland. Built using the Abt system, with additional gripper braking, the railway has carried passengers to the summit of Snowdon for over a century. Some original locomotives remain in use, but this 1923 example, 'Eryri', is no longer in service.

▲ Posted in 1908 to his mother by a young man on his first camping trip, this card shows a Talyllyn train at Tywyn. The caption, 'Toy Railway', indicates that the railway was by then dependent on holiday traffic rather than slate.

▼ A typical Snowdon train is a single carriage pushed up the line by a locomotive. Here, in the 1960s, two upward-bound trains wait in the loop at Clogwyn for a descending train to pass.

◄ The Ffestiniog Railway was always famous for the variety of its passenger coaches. This early 20th-century photograph shows a large guard's and luggage van, complete with a section for the carrying of dogs.

▲ This colourful 1970s card shows a busy day at Tan-y-Bwlch, an intermediate station and important passing point on the Ffestiniog Railway. Opened in 1836 to transport slate down to Porthmadog harbour, the line was originally gravity- and horse-operated. Steam arrived in 1863. Passenger traffic became important as the slate industry declined. It survived until 1946 and then in 1954 a long programme of restoration started to bring the railway back to life as a preserved line.

▲ This 1920s card and the coloured card (above right) show the Ffestiniog Railway's distinctive Fairlie double-boilered locomotives. Here, 'Merddin Emrys', built in 1879, waits with a train at Porthmadog. At this point the Ffestiniog Railway and the Welsh Highland Railway were both in operation and, thanks to the full restoration of the latter, they are again today.

▼ The Welshpool & Llanfair Light Railway opened in 1903 to serve predominantly local and rural needs. Passenger services ceased in 1931, but freight was still being carried in 1949, when this photograph was taken. Two of the railway's original locomotives, 'The Countess' and 'The Earl', stand in the yard at Welshpool, which by this time was part of the new British Railways network. The line was closed in 1956 but was subsequently reopened as a preserved railway. Both locomotives are still in use.

▶ The Corris Railway was opened in 1859 to connect the main line at Machynlleth with slate quarries around Corris, Aberllefenni and along the Dulas Valley. This 1920s photograph of a train standing at Machynlleth shows that, like so many other Welsh mineral lines, the Corris had by that time become dependent on passenger and holiday traffic. It closed in 1948, but sections have been restored and reopened.

▼ The Vale of Rheidol Railway was built in 1902 originally to serve lead mines and the timber trade. From the start, passenger and holiday traffic was important, and this has kept the railway running. It has passed through various owners, including Cambrian Railways, the GWR and British Railways, and is now operated as a preserved line. This 1970s photograph from the British Rail era shows a train at Aberystwyth headed by No. 9, 'Prince of Wales', which was built for the line by Cambrian Railways and is still in use today.

▼ Originally an early 19th-century horse-drawn tramway, the 4-mile line carrying clay from St Austell to Pentewan harbour, in Cornwall, was rebuilt in the 1870s for steam haulage. The railway also served other industries along the route, including the local gasworks. There was one passenger carriage, used by the railway's owners, the Hawkins family. The Pentewan railway closed in about 1916, but its route is now a footpath and cycleway. Traces are still in evidence, such as this weighbridge seen in 1992.

▲ When Magnus Volk's electric railway along the seafront in Brighton opened in 1883, it pioneered both electric power and the seaside miniature railway tradition. Today, the railway retains the atmosphere of the late Victorian era. Some early carriages are still in use, but the original 1883 vehicles were scrapped in the 1940s. Power is supplied via a third rail. This photograph was taken in the 1950s or 1960s, but it looks much the same today. It is the world's oldest operating electric railway.

▶ A short narrow gauge line was opened in about 1900 to connect the Penlee stone quarry, near Mousehole, with Newlyn quay. It was Cornwall's most westerly railway. Closed in 1973, it was replaced by a conveyor system, which in turn closed with the quarry in the late 1980s. Here, the 1954 Ruston Hornsby diesel locomotive 'J.W. Jenkin' draws loaded hoppers along the quay in June 1958. Then, quarry railways like this were in use all over Britain.

The Double Lift, Folkestone.

▶ Though not necessarily narrow gauge, the cliff railway was largely a creation of the same era as the passenger-carrying narrow gauge line, with popularity linked to the growth of tourism. Many were built in the Victorian and Edwardian eras, mostly in seaside towns where cliffs hindered beach access. About 25 are still in use. This early 20th-century card shows the famous double lift at Folkestone, opened in 1885 and duplicated in 1890. Today, only one lift remains.

LYNMOUTH. CLIFF LIFT

▲ The Lynton & Lynmouth Cliff Railway was opened in 1890, providing a vital link between the two towns and thereby encouraging their development as resorts. It was backed by the publisher Sir George Newnes, a local resident also instrumental in the building of the Lynton & Barnstaple narrow gauge railway. Water-powered and famously steep, the railway rises 500ft. This postcard dates from the 1930s.

▶ Hastings still has two cliff railways. This Edwardian card shows the East Hill Lift, soon after it was opened in 1903. Originally operated by a water-balance system, the line featured contrasting architectural styles, with a castle-like structure at the top and a cottage-style station at the bottom.

EAST HILL LIFT HASTINGS.

▲ The Aberystwyth Cliff Railway was opened in 1896. Originally water-operated, it was later converted to electric power. It is the longest cliff railway in Britain, and its winding route up Constitution Hill, often in rocky cuttings, and the magnificent views it offers over Cardigan Bay make the line one of the best in Britain. Despite this, it has had a chequered history, including periods of closure. This is a 1970s postcard.

INCIDENTS

ACCIDENTS AND DISASTERS have always been a feature of railway life, and many of the more serious have been documented – rather strangely, to modern eyes – by the issue of postcards and other commemorative material, particularly in the late Victorian and Edwardian eras. Less well known are the many minor incidents that have regularly occurred, generally as a result of human error. Some of these clearly had serious implications, especially for those involved, while others aroused the curiosity of passers-by or even provided entertainment for spectators. All the incidents shown here had an official enquiry.

▲ Accidents have occurred at level crossings since the early days of the railways, and the introduction of automatic gates and unmanned crossings only increased the risk of collision. This 1950s photograph shows the mangled remains of a van after a crash at Uckfield level crossing, in Sussex.

▲ This shows the result of a collision at Craigentinny, near Edinburgh, in December 1951. The damage to the Class V1 tank locomotive, No. 67630, looks serious and the first carriage has been derailed. Yet the driver is still in the cab, while two railwaymen and someone who looks like a passer-by are trying to carry out repairs.

▶ Storms in November 1951 washed away a section of a 30ft embankment near Midhurst, in Sussex. A Class C2X locomotive, No. 32522, and its tender fell into the gap, along with the leading coal wagon of its train. With ample supplies of fuel, the resulting fire burned for two weeks. The effects can be seen on the side of the cab. Luckily there were no casualties.

▼ Another breakdown crane, in this case a much larger one, rerails an elderly former Great Eastern Class J15 0-6-0 locomotive, No. 65475. The driver watches, and suited managers concentrate on directing the lift. The date is the late 1950s.

▲ This dramatic night-time shot shows a breakdown gang at work, trying to sort out a shunting locomotive that has derailed on the points. Flares light the scene as the men use jacks to rerail the GWR pannier tank. The setting is Hall Green goods yard near Birmingham, and the date is probably the 1960s. Minor incidents like this were once a regular feature of railway life, and were generally quickly resolved.

▼ In October 1988 two Class 31 diesels ended up on top of each other at Staples Corner on the North Circular Road in London, having run away out of control during shunting operations. Police, spectators and British Rail staff stand and stare.

▲ In this early 1920s incident, the breakdown crane has been summoned to recover a London, Brighton & South Coast Railway tank locomotive that seems to have overrun the buffers at the end of a siding. Police are in attendance, and there are plenty of spectators watching the drama.

SCOTLAND

PICTURE FILE

▲ Even the most familiar railway scenes warrant another look. Edinburgh's Waverley station must have been photographed thousands of times from this viewpoint but this summer 1955 version has plenty of interest. It is a steam-age scene but the platforms are surprisingly empty. The tracks, by contrast, are quite crowded, with several railwaymen wandering around.

▶ In this classic version of another much-photographed location, a former North British K Class 4-4-0 locomotive, now running as LNER Class 33 No. 9864, comes proudly off the Forth Bridge at the head of a local with a mixed bag of carriages. The date is the 1930s.

▼ In 1959 Fort William's original station, adjacent to Loch Linnhe, was still in use. Built as a terminus by the West Highland Railway in 1894, it was further developed with the opening of the extension to Mallaig in 1901. There was also a separate goods station. Everything was demolished when the new station was built in 1975. Watched by a few enthusiasts on the untidy platform, a Class 5MT, No. 44909, enters the station.

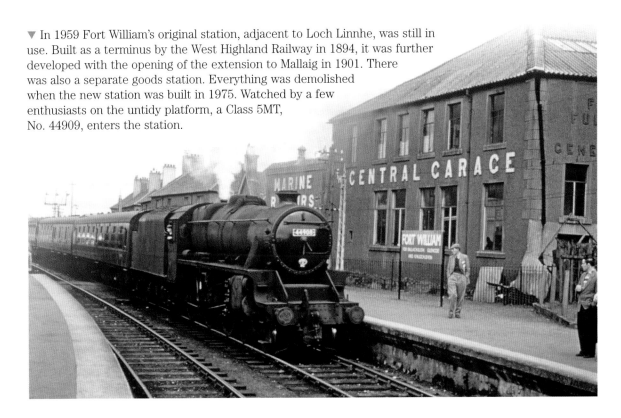

▲ A convenient bridge offered this photographer an interesting shot of another 5MT, No. 44794, as it slowed for the approach to Carmont, near Stonehaven, on the Montrose-to-Aberdeen line. The date is July 1966, and Scottish steam is disappearing.

▼ There were four locomotives called 'Cock o' the North'. This is the first, a North British 4-4-2 of 1911, seen here looking smart at Perth as LNER 9903, probably in the early 1930s. When the next one, a Gresley P2 2-8-2, went into service in 1934 as LNER 2001, this original 'Cock o' the North' was renamed 'Aberdonian'.

Scotland

◄ St Boswells, on the Waverley Route, was a busy station, the meeting point for several lines, as the nameboard indicates. Here, perhaps in the 1920s, an elderly tank locomotive rests in the platform, at the head of a short mixed goods. Advertisements promote trips to the west coast of Scotland, a long way from the Borders and their dense railway network – of which nothing exists today.

▼ In a scene expressive of country railways and branch lines all over Scotland, the single-coach, 4.05pm school train from Callander to Killin climbs slowly through Glen Ogle in 1960. The locomotive, No. 55263, is an LMS version of a Caledonian Railway design dating back to the 1890s. Within a few years, the entire local network of which this line was a part had been swept away.

▶ Another St Boswells view, this time on a cold morning in 1952 as A1 No. 60152, 'Holyrood', makes an impressive start under a clear blue sky.

Picture file

▼ While enthusiasts watch from the footbridge, LMS Jubilee No. 45588, 'Kashmir', stops at Castle Douglas in May 1963 with an enthusiasts' special, to be taken down the Kirkcudbright branch by a waiting tank locomotive. The Carlisle-based Jubilee looks immaculate.

▼ With plenty of steam and black smoke, a grimy-looking former LNER V2 Class locomotive, No. 60970, starts its mixed goods after a signal check at Riccarton Junction in 1962.

▼ Two ladies, wearing the distinctive style of the mid-1920s, have a serious conversation on the platform at Aberdeen, ignoring completely the former Great North of Scotland Class T locomotive standing quietly at the head of its goods train. The LNER took a number of these on, including No. 6902, reclassifying them as D41s.

Scotland

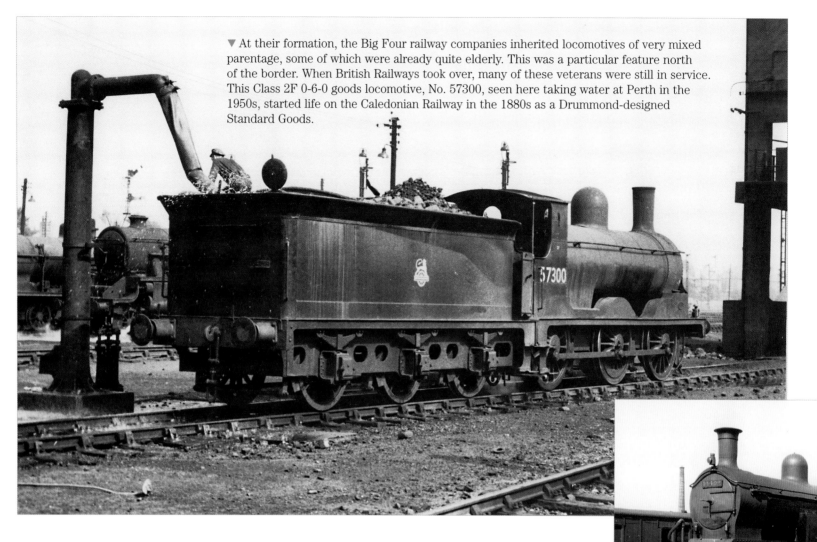

▼ At their formation, the Big Four railway companies inherited locomotives of very mixed parentage, some of which were already quite elderly. This was a particular feature north of the border. When British Railways took over, many of these veterans were still in service. This Class 2F 0-6-0 goods locomotive, No. 57300, seen here taking water at Perth in the 1950s, started life on the Caledonian Railway in the 1880s as a Drummond-designed Standard Goods.

◄ This Edwardian photograph shows a Highland Railway snowplough attached to a Class 18 locomotive, with three other class members coupled and ready for action. Dating from the 1860s, these are typical veterans retained for special duties.

Picture file

▶ The Glenfinnan Viaduct, on the line to Mallaig, is perennially popular with railway photographers. Taking pictures from a moving train is always difficult, but this image captured the atmosphere and the landscape. The date is 22 April 1978, the train is the 07.00 from Mallaig, and the locomotive is a Class 27 diesel, No. 27016.

▼ Another Scottish veteran, this former Highland Railway 4-4-0 passenger locomotive of the 1890s was one of a class of twenty known as 'Small Bens'. 'Ben Armin' is seen here in the 1930s as LMS No. 14402. This one was withdrawn in 1939, but some of the class survived into the British Railways era.

▼ Welded rails, in lengths of more than 400ft, were transported by rail from Motherwell to all parts of Scotland. This 1964 British Railways publicity photograph, issued when the idea of welded rails was still quite new, shows a typical load passing Langloan Junction, near Coatbridge.

▼ In the late 1940s and early 1950s, the Royal Scot was one of several long-distance expresses selected for trial haulage by the new Class 16/1 diesel-electric locomotives. Designed by the LMS but put into service by British Railways, these pioneering locomotives – the first mainline diesels in Britain – operated as a pair, as seen here.

LOST LINES

I have been lucky to have been able to explore Scotland's railway map, past and present, fairly thoroughly over the last twenty years. I have travelled most of the surviving lines, and my explorations of lost lines have taken me from the Solway Firth in the southwest to Lybster in the far north. The pursuit of lost lines is always enjoyable, albeit sometimes rather solitary, but it is probably at its best in Scotland, thanks to the richness, quality and diversity of the landscape.

Scotland suffered badly during the closures of the 1960s, losing main lines, now much missed, as well

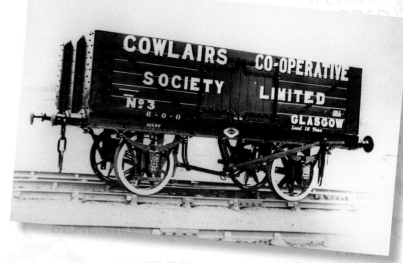

▲ Also lost is a vast fleet of private owner wagons. This example, seen fresh out of the paint shop in 1904, was owned by the Cowlairs Co-operative Society, a flourishing enterprise set up by railwaymen in 1881 in the Springburn area.

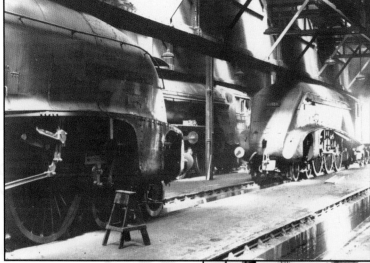

▲ 'Lost railways' usually means closed lines and abandoned stations, but it is easy to forget everything else that was lost in the process of closure. A prime example is the locomotive shed. This is Aberdeen's Ferryhill shed (61B) in July 1966, which was then housing such classics as a Class V2, No. 60813, and a pair of A4s, No. 60034, 'Lord Faringdon' and No. 60009, 'Union of South Africa'. The latter is preserved.

▼ This 1960s view of Dunfermline station is really about lost railways: there are no more mixed freights now, and the Edwardian Class J35 No. 64507, a survivor from the North British Railway, was cut up years ago.

▼ The Dundee & Newtyle Railway, opened in 1831, was one of the first in Scotland. This photograph, dating from 1962, shows a family group, perhaps a wedding party, posing on the platform on the old Newtyle station. The line closed a couple of years later but the station buildings survive, surrounded by houses.

◄▲ The Callander & Oban Railway opened its terminus at Oban in 1880. As seen in these 1930s photographs, it was a grand building in a decorative timber-framed style, marked by a clock tower (left) and boasting a train shed (above). In the 1980s the station was rebuilt on a much-reduced scale and all the old buildings, including the clock tower, were, despite being listed, demolished by British Rail.

▶ The 1860s line from Aberdeen northwards to Peterhead and Fraserburgh separated at Maud Junction. A substantial station, photographed in 2002, was built here, complete with turntable. This later became an important centre for cattle traffic. Passenger services ceased in 1965, while some freight continued until 1979.

▲ Knockando station was on the line from Aberdeen to Aviemore, which closed in 1968. In 2002 it was looking a bit sad but was later restored by the local whisky distillery, who renamed it Tamdhu after their brand and used it for a while as a shop.

▶ The most infamous and hotly opposed closure in Scotland was the Waverley Route from Edinburgh to Carlisle, which had been completed in the 1860s. After long legal battles, the line was closed in 1969. Here is a section near Galashiels a few years later, with the trackbed used as a car park. The section from here to Edinburgh is now being rebuilt as a railway.

as rural routes, and leaving large areas of the country without any kind of railway service. It could have been even worse, for the original Beeching closure plans included everything north of Inverness. The legacy is a wealth of lines to explore and photograph, many still hidden in the landscape awaiting the excitement of discovery by enthusiasts like me. Stations and structures survive in surprising quantities, mainly because there is so little pressure on the land. This also makes it easier than in the more densely populated areas of Britain to follow the dotted lines on the Ordnance Survey map, without the frustration of finding they have vanished under a new road or an industrial estate.

▼ The branch from Castle Douglas to Kirkcudbright was built through attractive Lowlands scenery. Opened in 1864, it closed 101 years later and its legacy is an easily explored route. Typical is this old embankment north of Kirkcudbright, with the remains of a bridge dwarfed by a tree that has grown up since the 1960s.

▼ Another significant loss was the direct line from Dumfries to Stranraer, the route of the Irish Mail via Castle Douglas and Newton Stewart. It too is a great line to explore. There is plenty left to find, including the eight delicate arches of Glenluce Viaduct, completed in 1861 to carry the line 78ft over the Water of Luce.

POSTERS & EPHEMERA

▲ Edinburgh: See Scotland by Rail – a BR Scottish Region poster of 1951 from a painting by J Berry

◀ Isle of Skye: First Class Hotels – an LNER poster of the mid-1930s from a painting by Schabelsky

▶ Oban – a Callander & Oban Railway poster of about 1910 (artist unknown)

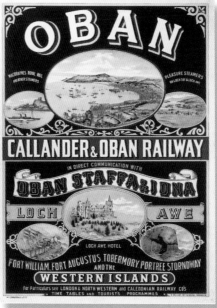

◀ Royal Deeside: It's Quicker by Rail – an LNER and LMS joint poster of 1937 from a painting by J McIntosh Patrick

▼ By Rail to the Highlands – a BR Scottish Region poster of the 1950s from a painting by Terence Cuneo

◀ St Andrews: The Home of the Royal & Ancient Game – an LNER poster of the 1930s from a painting by Henry Gawthorn

ADVANCE PROGRAMME
CIRCULAR TOURS
AND EXCURSIONS

SCOTLAND
TRAIN — MOTOR — STEAMER
SEASON 1956
BRITISH RAILWAYS

BRITISH RAILWAYS
SOUTHERN REGION   BR.21764/15

TO
SCOTTISH REGION

via   & Euston

The Journey Shrinker runs between London and Edinburgh.

Inter-City 125

GREAT
BRITAIN
and
NORTHERN
IRELAND

via STRANRAER and LARNE

THE SHORT SEA ROUTE
70 MINUTES
open sea passage

6th JUNE until
14th SEPTEMBER, 1958

BRITISH RAILWAYS

From 9 April to
LO
to
GLASGOW

STA
SP
7

★ STAY
★ EXPRESS
★ NIGHT BU
★ FARE INCLU
★ ADVANCE BOO

Full det

Glasgow and South-Western Ry
TO
EDINBURGH
WAVERLEY, N.B.
FROM
AYR

▲▼▶ Efficient, high-speed travel between London and Scotland was the aim of railway companies in the Victorian period, and subsequent generations of publicity offices, from British Rail's InterCity to the more independent ScotRail, have maintained its promotion. Also important throughout the same period has been the promotion of ferry services to Ireland, which for many people offered a longer rail journey balanced by a short sea route.

BRITISH RAIL   BR 2188

ABERDEEN

All in Holiday
IN BONNIE
SCOTLAND
TOUR N° 1. GLASGOW & DUNOON · TOUR N° 2. DUNOON & EDINBURGH | With Sight Seeing Tours

EACH SATURDAY
10TH JUNE TO 9TH SEPT.
RETURNING THE FOLLOWING SATURDAY

£15. 15. 0
CHILDREN UNDER 14 £10. 10. 0

NO EXTRAS

INCLUSIVE OF RAIL FARE. MEALS ON TRAINS
ACCOMMODATION, SIGHT-SEEING TOURS & GRATUITIES
FULL DETAILS & BOOKING FORMS from STATIONS AND AGENCIES

THE CLYDE

A day in the Central Highlands

TOUR No.II

LOCH TAY DAY TOUR

by train to Aberfeldy, motor coach to Killin via Loch Tay and train home
(or the route may be reversed)

DAILY (except Sundays)

15th June to 29th August, 1964

Loch Tay and Ben Lawers

FARES FOR THE ROUND

From	1st Class	2nd Class
DUNBLANE	32/-	22/9
DUNDEE (West or Tay Bridge)	40/9	28/9
DUNKELD	32/-	22/9
EDINBURGH (Waverley)	45/3	31/9
FALKIRK (Grahamston)	39/-	27/6
GLASGOW (Buchanan Street)	43/-	30/-
GRANGEMOUTH	39/9	28/-
LARBERT	38/3	27/-
PERTH	32/-	22/9
PITLOCHRY	35/-	24/9
STIRLING	34/6	24/6

TICKETS OBTAINABLE IN ADVANCE

at Stations and accredited Rail Ticket Agencies and are valid on the date for which issued and by the services specified.

All information regarding tours, excursions and cheap fares will be supplied on application at stations or to—
J. Coward, District Passenger Manager, 87 Union Street, Glasgow, C.I. Telephone City 2911.
J. K. Cumming, District Commercial Manager, 87 Union Street, Glasgow, C.I. Telephone City 2911.
A. Haworth, District Commercial Manager, 23 Waterloo Place, Edinburgh, Telephone Waverley 2477.
or R. Gemmell, District Traffic [illegible] Dundee. [illegible] Telephone 26835.

September 1954

N to EDINBURGH

5 DAYS
T TRAVEL
S AVAILABLE
ESERVED SEAT
ARE ESSENTIAL

LNER O. 6013
19
From Stainby Ironstone Sidings

TO MOTHERWELL
L M S. Rly.   CALE Secn
Via Donc. York Berwick N.B. & Whifflet
Owner and No. of Wagon
2
Sheets in or on Wagon
Consignee Colvilles Iron & Steel Works

THE ABERDONIAN

ABERDEEN
via
Darlington
Newcastle
Kirkcaldy
Arbroath
Stonehaven
Edinburgh
Dundee
Montrose

E

YOUR SCOTRAIL EXPRESS RAIL GUIDE

16 May until 2 October 1988.

GLASGOW · EDINBURGH · DUNDEE
ABERDEEN · INVERNESS

≷ ScotRail

L.N.E.R.   B 877

LUGGAGE

From MELROSE

To LEVEN

Railways

20 JUN 1964

Castle Mail, Kyleakin.

DAY TOUR No 19
from FORT WILLIAM and other stations in the LOCHABER area

BY TRAIN—MOTOR COACH—STEAMER

Tickets obtainable in advance at stations and are valid on the date for which issue

Children under three years of age, free; three years and under fourteen, half-fare.

All information regarding Tours, Excursions and Cheap Fares will be supplied on application at stations or to the Divisional Manager, 87 Union Street, Glasgow, C.I. Telephone CIty 2911

≷ British Rail

George Outram & Co. Ltd., Perth

◀ ▼ ▲ Scottish tourism became increasingly important in the 20th century as a way to create revenue and keep in business a complex network of both main lines and rural routes. The emphasis was on tours and excursions, particularly during the 1950s and 1960s. At the same time, the importance of freight traffic on Scottish lines should not be forgotten, with the railways being the prime mover of bulk cargoes such as coal.

Est. 760. 5,000. 8/27.   M 9801

L.N.E.R.
LUGGAGE.
From
To **GLASGOW**

No. 2   NORTH BRITISH RAILWAY—COAL WAY-BILL

From **BALGONIE COLLIERY,**
To Methil
Per ____ Station, via ____
____ o'clock Train   6/11 1895 Arrived ____ 189

[handwritten tabular coal weights and figures, including "M Taggart & Boy", "Coal", "282.11", "yds for shift"]

RAILWAY POSTCARDS

Loch Awe and Kilchern Castle

1. LNWR 'official card' of Loch Awe and Kilchern Castle c.1910

2. View of Loch Lomond and West Highland Line c.1910

3. Edinburgh's Caledonian Station Hotel interior c.1920

4. LNWR 'official card' of Oban posted in 1907

5. 1922 card of a Glasgow & South Western Railway 4-6-4 locomotive

6. Edwardian view of a Caledonian Railway express near Glasgow Central

7. 1950s card of a BR Scottish Region A4 Pacific locomotive and Aberdeen express

8. Edwardian view of the Station Hotel, Dumfries

9. 1920s view of the Tay Bridge from the south

41823. WEST HIGHLAND RAILWAY, LOCH LOMOND.

THE DINING ROOM
CALEDONIAN STATION HOTEL
EDINBURGH

Oban.

G & S W R

BRITISH RAILWAYS. *SCOTTISH REGION.* This east coast Aberdeen express is skirting the northern bank of the Firth of Forth. The Forth Bridge can be seen in the distance. The locomotive is one of the famous Gresley A4 Streamline Pacific Class.

B. 30316. DUMFRIES: STATION H

DUMFRIES

TAY BRIDGE DUNDEE, from S. Longest bridge in the World. Total Cost £650000. Length of viaduct 10780 Feet.

ENTHUSIASTS

THERE HAVE been railway enthusiasts right from the birth of the railways, and luckily many of them have also been photographers. Some are well known but, sadly, many are anonymous. Their legacy is a rich pictorial archive of railway history. Included in it is a large collection of photographs of enthusiasts, offering an intriguing insight into the enduring appeal of the train, and notably the steam train, especially among boys and young men of all ages. They also reflect a more relaxed era, free from modern Health and Safety concerns.

▼ A great enthusiast and a key name in railway photography is Henry Cecil Casserley. Here he is seen in 1946, posing for someone else's camera in front of a GWR veteran during a shed tour.

▼ In 1955 the local railway history society visited Loughborough's Derby Road shed, and were recorded on camera with an old LMS Class 4F, No. 44148. The members of the group are all named on the back of the photograph. The lady is called Millie Mason.

▲ John Goss is a well-known enthusiast and railway photographer who for nearly 30 years worked in the British Rail Photographic Unit. Here, in the late 1960s, perched precariously on a decrepit pallet on top of a forklift truck, he is busy photographing the vast floorspace of the Hither Green Continental Freight Terminal.

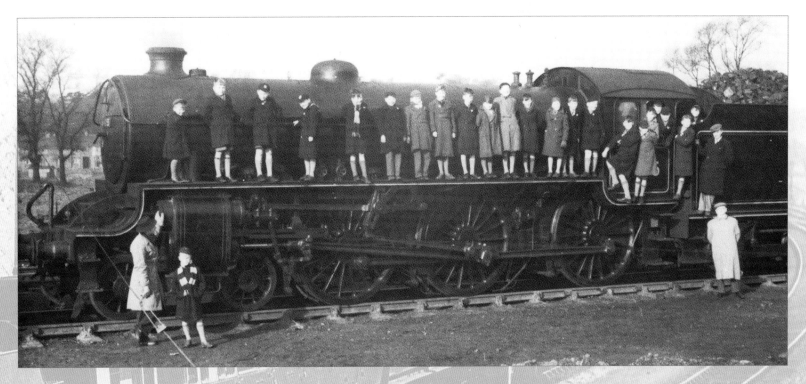

▲This delightful 1950s photograph records a shed outing by a school railway enthusiasts' group. All but one of the boys, in classic gaberdine macs, caps and shorts, have been lined up on the locomotive, while their teachers have remained safely on the ground.

▼The centenary of George Stephenson's death was celebrated widely in Northeast England in 1948. There was an exhibition at the Laing Art Gallery, Newcastle-upon-Tyne, along with several railway displays. This one, clearly enjoyed by families, was by Market Place station in Chesterfield. The locomotive, former Great Central Director Class locomotive No. 62658, 'Prince George', looks smart in new British Railways livery but, built in 1913, it was hardly the latest thing.

▲ Railtours were an increasingly common enthusiast activity from the 1950s. This is Broad Street, London, in May 1958. An RCTS special, headed by an N7 Class tank locomotive, No. 69632, rests in the platform while a group of typical enthusiasts have a serious-looking discussion with the driver.

▲ Railway enthusiasts tend to be meticulous record keepers. This photograph of a suburban service hauled by a Stanier-designed 3MT tank locomotive still with its old LMS livery is signed by the photographer, GP Mitchell, dated 14 October 1950 and inscribed on the mount with full camera details, including the developer he had used.

◄ Another railtour, this time an LCGB special, waits at Millwall Junction, East London, in May 1956. The locomotive, Class 2F No. 58859, is a Victorian veteran dating from 1880. The passengers throng the platform, while one elderly chap leans back to enjoy the view from the other side while his friend takes the photograph.

▶ Enthusiasts taking part in an RCTS railtour in March 1958 wander about all over the tracks in the sidings controlled by Deptford Wharf North signal box. The photographer has noted some things not to be missed, including the bell on the signal box, folding crossing gates and an 'E6 on unfitted freight'.

▼ Also in the 1950s, a group of Severn Venturer railtour enthusiasts enjoy the sunshine on the platform of a very decorative but closed station while their locomotive, a former GWR saddle tank, surrounds itself with steam.

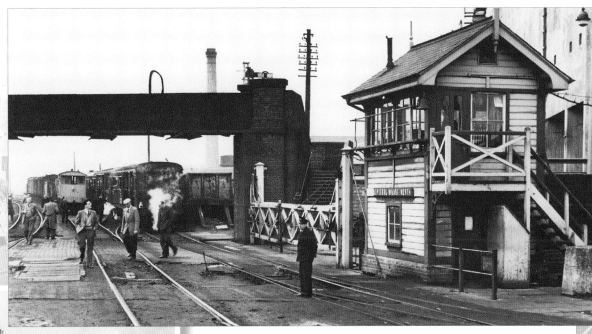

▼ In the summer of 1953 enthusiasts packed the platforms at London King's Cross to watch the smoky departure of a double-headed special bound for Doncaster. The leading locomotive, No. 990, 'Henry Oakley', is the first of the GNR's C1 Klondyke Class, introduced from 1898. The first Atlantic-type locomotives in Britain, the Klondykes were designed by Henry Ivatt. At that time, No. 990 was the sole survivor of the class, and today it is still part of the national collection.

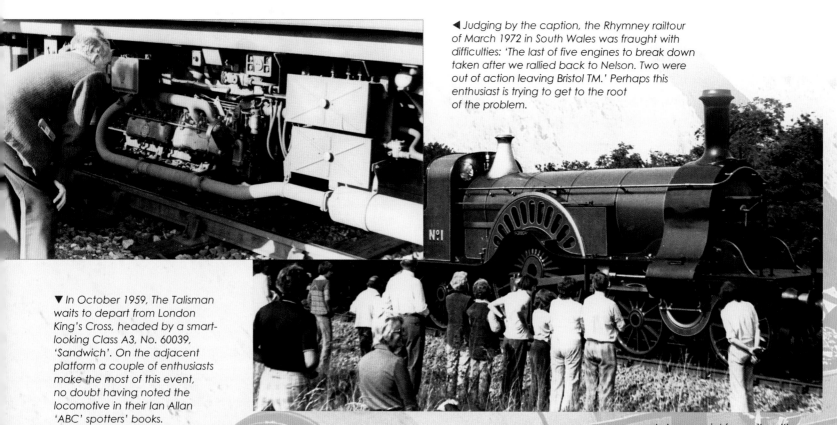

◀ Judging by the caption, the Rhymney railtour of March 1972 in South Wales was fraught with difficulties: 'The last of five engines to break down taken after we rallied back to Nelson. Two were out of action leaving Bristol TM.' Perhaps this enthusiast is trying to get to the root of the problem.

▼ In October 1959, The Talisman waits to depart from London King's Cross, headed by a smart-looking Class A3, No. 60039, 'Sandwich'. On the adjacent platform a couple of enthusiasts make the most of this event, no doubt having noted the locomotive in their Ian Allan 'ABC' spotters' books.

▲ A perennial favourite with enthusiasts is GNR No.1, the first of the famous Stirling Singles, and one of the all-time classic designs. Here, the locomotive is enjoying a typical response from onlookers at an outing in the late 1960s.

SPOTTINGS and JOTTINGS

The official organ of the Ian Allan Locospotters Club

| No. 1 | AUGUST, 1948 | 1d. |

Locospotters—Your own Journal!

WE now present you with your own journal—exclusively and absolutely yours. This new four-page broadsheet is to be devoted entirely to the Ian Allan Locospotters Club, its rallies, its visits, and all its other activities, and articles on ancient matters and high technicalities are strictly barred.

We are running this paper to stimulate your interest. We hope that you will enter for the competitions, send us your photographs, and write to us on any interesting points.

To avoid confusion with the original "spotters" who did some splendid work during the war identifying aircraft we have changed the name of the club to the "Ian Allan Locospotters Club." The word "Locospotters" is now our own title, and one which cannot be legitimately used other than by members of our Club.

Spottings and Jottings will appear roughly four times a year, and a copy will be included with each issue of 'Trains Illustrated.' If you are not a subscriber to Trains Illustrated, you can receive *Spottings and Jottings* from the

Spotters' Club Secretary, or from the North Western area Mail Order Department at Berkhamsted.

'Spotters Visit R.H. & D.R.

The world's smallest public railway ran the world's longest smallest train on June 5th, when 250 locospotters, travelling in 24 coaches, hauled by two engines, enjoyed the freedom of the R.H. & D.R.

Special carriages conveyed the party from London to New Romney, where a visit was paid to Model-land, in which there is an elaborate O gauge model railway.

The party then travelled to Hythe and back to Dungeness for tea, returning to New Romney to catch a special train back to London.

R. H. & D. Hurricane on the Spot!

▲ Preserved railways offer ample opportunities for enthusiasts to get their hands dirty. Here, on the South Devon Railway, probably in the 1970s, a girl and a young boy pause from their polishing duties to smile at the camera. The locomotive, a 1934 GWR Class 6400, no. 6412, is much travelled, having spent time at several preserved lines, including the North Norfolk, the West Somerset and the Gloucestershire Warwickshire.

▲ In this early 1960s scene, the driver of Princess Coronation Class No. 46256, 'Sir William A Stanier FRS', looks at his watch, ignored by the two elderly enthusiasts, deep in conversation. Meanwhile, the boy waits politely, but a bit uneasily, and fidgets with his feet, perhaps uncomfortable in his winkle-pickers.

▶ This small boy, smart in school uniform and posing stiffly for the camera, must have had a wonderful time at this shed somewhere in the LMS region. He is dwarfed by the old MR 3F 0-6-0 standing behind him, which even then was a veteran.

◀ Ian Allan's 'ABC' guides had been essential reading for enthusiasts since the early 1940s. Next came the Ian Allan Locospotters Club, and the launch in August 1948 of the Club journal, Spottings and Jottings.

Index

Chapter opener illustrations

Pages 8–9 In August 1967 an engineering train comes slowly into Shap station, hauled by a British Rail standard locomotive running tender first. A year later Shap closed to passengers.

Pages 74–5 In its last years, steam still produced great pictures: in April 1966 West Country Class No. 34006, 'Bude', races through Devon countryside on its way to Sidmouth with a special tour to Bicton Gardens.

Pages 100–1 The ordinary scenes of daily railway life acquire interest with time: A Portsmouth-to-Waterloo EMU approaches Guildford in May 1975. Now, all slam-door trains have gone, along with the Minis seen in the car park.

Pages 126–7 In the 1950s, scenes like this were part of daily life in Wales: a GWR Class 7400 saddle tank locomotive takes a typical mixed freight across the Tywi near Carmarthen, under a fine signal gantry.

Pages 150–1 Opened in 1905 to serve a small village, Stewartby station was soon surrounded by one of England's largest brickworks. This produced up to 700 million bricks a year and was served by a huge complex of sidings. Brickworks and chimneys are gone, but the station lives on.

Pages 178–9 Steam was an integral part of the industrial scene: while enthusiasts watch, a Class 8F 2-8-0 takes a heavy ballast train across the March line, south of Peterborough, in May 1963.

Pages 202–3 Traditionally, the railway companies were keen on geography, and liked to mark important boundaries. The LNER erected this boundary marker on the Tyne Bridge in the 1930s.

Pages 228–9 It is hard to take good photographs from moving trains, but this 1960s view of a Fort William-to-Mallaig train is very successful and places the train perfectly into the surrounding Scottish landscape.

AUTHOR'S ACKNOWLEDGEMENTS

In the course of producing our sequence of railway books, of which this is the latest, thousands of photographs, postcards and pieces of railway ephemera have been used. Many were acquired for particular purposes, and used accordingly, while others I bought simply because I found them interesting. There was always the hope that their time would come. This book, taking as it does a more personal approach, has been an opportunity to bring many of these out of their boxes and into the light of day.

Their diversity, and the captions they inspired, have been a challenge to both Sue Gordon, my ever-patient editor, and Dawn Terrey, my clever designer, both of whom must now know a thing or two about trains. I am indebted to them for their constant enthusiasm and support. As ever, I am grateful to my wife Chrissie, for her ability to work her way without complaint through hundreds of images, and make them all better, and for her tolerance of yet another railway book dominating our lives for months.

I owe particular thanks to Barry Jones, Tony Harden, Gavin Morrison and Michael Mensing, all of whom could always be relied upon to find things from their collections to fill those difficult gaps. Many other friends and colleagues from the railway world have been generous with their time and encouragement. Charles Allenby, Julian Holland and Bob Compton have been meticulous in checking the text, and correcting my many mistakes. Geoff King, David M Stacey and Jean Lucas have made available special photographs. Last, but not least, my gratitude to Richard and Judi Furness is considerable, for their kindness and generosity in giving me the use of wonderful posters from the *Poster to Poster* collection.

PICTURE CREDITS

Photographs used in this book have come from many sources. Some have been supplied by photographers or picture libraries, while others have been bought on the open market. In the latter case, photographers or libraries have been acknowledged whenever possible. However, many such images inevitably remain anonymous, despite attempts at tracing or identifying their origin. If photographs or images have been used without due credit or acknowledgement, through no fault of our own, apologies are offered. If you believe this is the case, please let us know because we would like to give full credit in any future edition.

Unless otherwise specified, all archive photographs and postcards are from the author's collection.
l = left; r = right; t = top; b = bottom; m = middle

Photographs by Paul Atterbury
10bl; 12ml; 12tr; 12br; 13br; 17br; 19b; 38br; 39tl; 39br; 40t; 42tl; 48b; 49t; 63tl; 83tl; 83bl; 83br; 84bl; 85tl; 85br; 108br; 109b; 111tl; 111tr; 111b; 134mr; 134b; 186t; 187b; 188t; 188b; 189tr; 189br; 211ml; 211br; 212mr; 213t; 239t; 239b

Other images
Allen, Ian C: 182b
Aston, JH: 23br; 97tr; 200bl; 224b
Ballantyne, HB: 24bl
Beal, Peter: 227br
Bennett, Alex M: 52b
Bennett, M: 206t
Blencowe, SV: 130tr; 132tl; 135tl; 137t; 237t
Bowman, John J: 133tl; 155tl; 235t
Brockhurst, RB: 211tr
Bryan, Melvyn: 69t
Carr, IS: 11tl; 204tr; 206mr
Casserley, HC: 22tr; 25tr; 152tl; 181t; 183tl; 234mr
Coles, CRL: 105tr; 145br; 183b; 249b
Colour Rail: 7tl
Connolly, K: 59bl; 77mr; 107b; 209tl
Conolly, P: 61mr
Cook, KL: 16b; 105ml
Creer, Stanley: 10tr; 185b
Davies Hugh, 104m
Dobson, PA: 156mr
Dodson, Nick: 13ml
Dunnett, M: 147bl; 208tl
Dyckhoff, NFW: 58b
Edwards Brian: 81t; 156tl; 156b
Elsey, L: 78b
Esau, Mike: 19tr
Eychenne, Alfred: 198bl
Field, K: 123mr; 146t; 146b; 204b; 205b; 208tr

Foster, H: 120b
Foster, PR: 92b
Frost, ARJ: 181br
Gammell, C: 22bl; 85tr; 248t; 248b
Garth, WS: 221b
Gates, FM: 126–7
Gillam, JG: 104t
Glover, JG: 100–1; 157t
Goss, John: 20m; 21b; 63tr; 74–5; 79t; 128br; 145l; 147t; 209b
Grant, DA: 64br
Green, CC: 227tl
Gregory: 136mr
Griffiths, D: 11br; 77t
Groom, PH: 153tr
Hamblin, Donald: 63ml
Harden, Tony: 14tl; 14bl; 14mr; 15ml; 17bl; 18ml; 18mr; 19tl; 19br (inset); 26–7t; 27tr; 27mr; 28tr; 28br; 29bl; 29tr; 30tl; 30bl; 30br; 31tl; 31tr; 31br; 32–3t; 33tm; 34tl; 34tr; 34br; 35ml; 36–7m; 36–7b; 38tl; 38bl; 39bl; 40mr; 40b; 42tr; 43t; 44tl; 44br; 46mr; 48ml; 51tl; 51tr; 52tr; 53t; 53b; 54bl; 55tl; 82tr; 83tr; 84tr; 84br; 85bl; 108ml; 109tl; 109ml; 109tr; 186mr; 187t; 187m; 189tl; 189bl
Hardman, J: 235b
Haydon, JC: 105b
Heavyside, Tom: 133bl; 208b
Heiron, GF: 173b
Hepburn, TG: 41b; 58tr; 66b; 231b; 233b

Hillmer, JC: 59m
Hocquard, P: 65bl; 231tr
Hogarth, P: 205t
Hoole, K: 48t
Hopwood, HL: 85ml
Household, HGW: 182ml
Jackson, LH: 107tl
James, H: 181b; 247t
Joyce, M: 250b
Kemp, HC: 183ml
Kerr, FR: 69br
King, Geoff: 158–61 (all)
Lapper, LB: 26bl
Lee, J: 97m
Leech, Kenneth: 171b
Mann, JD: 185tr
Mensing, Michael: 32b; 33bl; 33br; 35b; 36tl; 36ml; 37t; 42br; 43b; 44bl; 45br; 46tl; 46bl; 47tl; 47mr; 49bl; 153b
Mitchell, GP: 248mr
Morrison, Gavin: 50b; 51b; 54t; 54mr; 55mr;
Morten, E: 153mr
Mortimer, GR: 57b; 184t
Moss, FF: 80bl
Nicolle, Barry J: 64bl
Oldham, CPH: 180t
Ord, C: 210b
Plant, C: 95b
Pope, M: 207tl
Ralston, W: 119t

Rickard, S: 130br
Riley, RC: 78t; 93b; 130tl; 154tl; 154b; 173t
Roberts, Jonathan: 246tr
Roberts, RF: 2–3
Robinson, Gerald T: 63b; 71t; 104b; 178–9
Ross, MA: 47b
Russell-Smith, JF: 76b
Sawford, Eric: 94tl; 99b; 131b; 227mr; 234t
Scrace, J: 103t
Siviter, REB: 131ml
Spencer-Gilks, T: 128bl
Stacey, David M: 84tl
Stanton, Anne: 13tl
Stead, NE: 49br; 213b; 236b
Thompson, Douglas: 45mr; 186b; 212tl; 212b
Treacy Eric: 10ml; 72b
Turner, Mike: 8–9; 206b
Turner, Raymond: 184m
Verden Anderson, WJ: 232b
Vincent, RE: 77b
Wagstaff, John: 7bl
Watkins, B: 68br; 81b; 209tr
Wilkins, Stephen: 184b
Williams, TE: 79b

256